To my

~love
you!
Love, Stacy '94

MW00977531

To
MOTHER

AN ANTHOLOGY OF MOTHER VERSE

Most of all the other
beautiful things in life
come by twos and threes
by dozens and hundreds
Plenty of roses, stars
sunsets, rainbows
brothers and sisters
aunts and cousins
but only one Mother
in all the wide world

TO MOTHER

An Anthology of Mother Verse

LONGMEADOW
P R E S S

1994

A Platinum Press Book

This special reprint edition originally
published in 1917 is now republished by:

Longmeadow Press
201 High Ridge Road
Stamford CT 06904

in association with

Platinum Press Inc.
311 Crossways Park Drive
Woodbury, NY 11797

ISBN 0-681-00601-3

0987654321

Printed in the USA

Library of Congress Cataloging-in-Publication Data

To mother : an anthology of mother verse.
        p. cm.
    Originally published : Boston : Houghton Mifflin,1917.
    "A Platinum Press book."
    Includes indexes.
    ISBN (invalid) 187958206
    1. Mothers — Poetry.   2. Motherhood — Poetry
3. English poetry. 4. American poetry.
PR1195.M63T6 1994
821.008'03520431—dc20   93-45716
                                                    CIP

To My Mother

God gives us friends—and that means much;
    But far above all others,
The greatest of his gifts to earth
    Was when He thought of Mothers

FOREWORD

SCATTERED throughout the works of the great poets, there are many beautiful tributes to mothers and subtle interpretations of motherhood; also, in old as well as in very new poems, there are illuminating suggestions to mothers regarding both their opportunities and their responsibilities. This valuable body of "mother literature" has but one drawback — the fact that it is so diffused. The aim of this book has been to gather together in one volume the very best poems from these various sources, for the use and also for the enjoyment of present-day mothers, both young and old.

CONTENTS

Contents

Contents

Contents

The YOUNG MOTHER

SEVEN TIMES FOUR

Heigh ho ! daisies and buttercups,
   Fair yellow daffodils, stately and tall,
When the wind wakes how they rock in the
     grasses,
   And dance with the cuckoo-buds, slender
     and small :
Here's two bonny boys, and here's mother's
     own lasses,
   Eager to gather them all.

Heigh ho ! daisies and buttercups,
   Mother shall thread them a daisy chain ;
Sing them a song of the pretty hedge-spar-
     row,
   That loved her brown little ones, loved
     them full fain ;
Sing, " Heart thou art wide though the house
     be but narrow " —
   Sing once, and sing it again.

Heigh ho ! daisies and buttercups,
   Sweet wagging cowslips, they bend and
     they bow ;
A ship sails afar over warm ocean waters,
   And haply one musing doth stand at her
     prow.

To Mother

O bonny brown sons, and O sweet little
    daughters,
  Maybe he thinks on you now!

Heigh ho! daisies and buttercups,
  Fair yellow daffodils stately and tall;
A sunshiny world full of laughter and leisure,
  And fresh hearts unconscious of sorrow
    and thrall,
Send down on their pleasure smiles passing
    its measure —
  God that is over us all.

Jean Ingelow

A MOTHER'S PICTURE

SHE seemed an angel to our infant eyes!
Once, when the glorifying moon revealed
Her who at evening by our pillow kneeled —
Soft-voiced and golden-haired, from holy
    skies
Flown to her loves on wings of Paradise —
We looked to see the pinions half-concealed.
The Tuscan vines and olives will not yield
Her back to me, who loved her in this
    wise,
And since have little known her, but have
    grown
To see another mother, tenderly,
Watch over sleeping darlings of her own;

4

The Young Mother

Perchance the years have changed her: yet
    alone
This picture lingers: still she seems to me
The fair, young Angel of my infancy.
           Edmund Clarence Stedman

MOTHER'S LOVE

HE sang so wildly, did the Boy,
That you could never tell
If 't was a madman's voice you heard,
Or if the spirit of a bird
Within his heart did dwell:
A bird that dallies with his voice
Among the matted branches;
Or on the free blue air his note
To pierce, and fall, and rise, and float,
With bolder utterance launches,
None ever was so sweet as he,
The boy that wildly sang to me;
Though toilsome was the way and long,
He led me not to lose the song.

But when again we stood below
The unhidden sky, his feet
Grew slacker, and his note more slow,
But more than doubly sweet.
He led me then a little way
Athwart the barren moor,
And then he stayed and bade me stay

To Mother

Beside a cottage door;
I could have stayed of mine own will,
In truth, my eye and heart to fill
With the sweet sight which I saw there,
At the dwelling of the cottager.

A little in the doorway sitting,
The mother plied her busy knitting,
And her cheek so softly smiled,
You might be sure, although her gaze
Was on the meshes of the lace,
Yet her thoughts were with her child.
But when the boy had heard her voice,
As o'er her work she did rejoice,
His became silent altogether,
And slily creeping by the wall
He seiz'd a single plume, let fall
By some wild bird of longest feather;
And all a-tremble with his freak,
He touch'd her lightly on the cheek.

Oh, what a loveliness her eyes
Gather in that one moment's space,
While peeping round the post she spies
Her darling's laughing face!
Oh, mother's love is glorifying,
On the cheek like sunset lying;
In the eyes a moisten'd light,
Softer than the moon at night!

Thomas Burbidge

THE WIDOW'S MITE

A WIDOW, — she had only one!
A puny and decrepit son;
   But, day and night,
Though fretful oft, and weak and small,
A loving child, he was her all, —
   The Widow's Mite.

The Widow's Mite — aye, so sustain'd,
She battled onward, nor complain'd
   Though friends were fewer:
And while she toil'd for daily fare,
A little crutch upon the stair
   Was music to her.

I saw her then, and now I see
That, though resign'd and cheerful, she
   Has sorrow'd much:
She has, — He gave it tenderly, —
Much faith, and, carefully laid by,
   A little crutch.
          Frederick Locker-Lampson

THE DAGUERREOTYPE

THIS, then, is she,
My mother as she looked at seventeen,
When she first met my father. Young in-
   credibly,

7

To Mother

Younger than spring, without the faintest
    trace
Of disappointment, weariness, or tear
Upon the childlike earnestness and grace
Of the waiting face.
Those close-wound ropes of pearl
(Or common beads made precious by their
    use)
Seem heavy for so slight a throat to wear;
But the low bodice leaves the shoulders bare
And half the glad swell of the breast, for news
That now the woman stirs within the girl.
And yet,
Even so, the loops and globes
Of beaten gold
And jet
Hung, in the stately way of old,
From the ears' drooping lobes
On festivals and Lord's-day of the week,
Show all too matron-sober for the cheek, —
Which, now I look again, is perfect child,
Or no — or no — 't is girlhood's very self,
Moulded by some deep, mischief-ridden elf
So meek, so maiden mild,
But startling the close gazer with the sense
Of passion forest-shy and forest-wild,
And delicate delirious merriments.

As a moth beats sidewise
And up and over, and tries

The Young Mother

To skirt the irresistible lure
Of the flame that has him sure,
My spirit, that is none too strong to-day,
Flutters and makes delay, —
Pausing to wonder at the perfect lips,
Lifting to muse upon the low-drawn hair
And each hid radiance there,
But powerless to stem the tide-race bright,
The vehement peace which drifts it toward
        the light
Where soon — ah, now, with cries
Of grief and giving-up unto its gain
It shrinks no longer nor denies,
But dips
Hurriedly home to the exquisite heart of
        pain, —
And all is well, for I have seen them plain,
The unforgettable, the unforgotten eyes!
Across the blinding gush of these good tears
They shine as in the sweet and heavy years
When by her bed and chair
We children gathered jealously to share
The sunlit aura breathing myrrh and thyme,
Where the sore-stricken body made a clime
Gentler than May and pleasanter than rhyme,
Holier and more mystical than prayer.
God, how thy ways are strange!
That this should be, even this,
The patient head
Which suffered years ago the dreary change!

To Mother

That these so dewy lips should be the same
As those I stooped to kiss
And heard my harrowing half-spoken name,
A little ere the one who bowed above her,
Our father and her very constant lover,
Rose stoical, and we knew that she was dead.
Then I, who could not understand or share
His antique nobleness,
Being unapt to bear
The insults which time flings us for our
          proof,
Fled from the horrible roof
Into the alien sunshine merciless,
The shrill satiric fields ghastly with day
Raging to front God in his pride of sway
And hurl across the lifted swords of fate
That ringed Him where He sat
My puny gage of scorn and desolate hate
Which somehow should undo Him, after
          all!
That this girl face, expectant, virginal,
Which gazes out at me
Boon as a sweetheart, as if nothing loth
(Save for the eyes, with other presage
          stored)
To pledge me troth,
And in the kingdom where the heart is lord
Take sail on the terrible gladness of the
          deep
Whose winds the gray Norns keep, —

The Young Mother

That this should be indeed
The flesh which caught my soul, a flying
　　　seed,
Out of the to and fro
Of scattering hands where the seedsman
　　　Mage,
Stooping from star to star and age to age
Sings as he sows!
That underneath this breast
Nine moons I fed
Deep of divine unrest,
While over and over in the dark she said,
" Blessed! but not as happier children
　　　blessed " —
That this should be
Even she . . .
God, how with time and change
Thou makest thy footsteps strange!
Ah, now I know
They play upon me, and it is not so
Why, 't is a girl I never saw before,
A little thing to flatter and make weep,
To tease until her heart is sore,
Then kiss and clear the score;
A gypsy run-the-fields,
A little liberal daughter of the earth,
Good for what hour of truancy and mirth
The careless season yields
Hither-side the flood of the year and yonder
　　　of the neap;

To Mother

Then thank you, thanks again, and twenty
      light good-byes, —
O shrined above the skies,
Frown not, clear brow,
Darken not, holy eyes!
Thou knowest well I know that it is thou
Only to save from such memories
As would unman me quite,
Here in this web of strangeness caught
And prey to troubled thought
Do I devise
These foolish shifts and slight;
Only to shield me from the afflicting sense
Of some waste influence
Which from this morning face and lustrous
      hair
Breathes on me sudden ruin and despair.
In any other guise,
With any but this girlish depth of gaze,
Your coming had not so unsealed and
      poured
The dusty amphoras where I had stored
The drippings of the winepress of my days.
I think these eyes foresee,
Now in their unawakened virgin time,
Their mother's pride in me,
And dream even now, unconsciously,
Upon each soaring peak and sky-hung lea
You pictured I should climb.
Broken premonitions come,

The Young Mother

Shapes, gestures visionary,
Not as once to maiden Mary
The manifest angel with fresh lilies came
Intelligibly calling her by name;
But vanishingly, dumb,
Thwarted and bright and wild,
As heralding a sin-defiled,
Earth-encumbered, blood-begotten, passion-
    ate man-child,
Who yet should be a trump of mighty call
Blown in the gates of evil kings
To make them fall;
Who yet should be a sword of flame before
The soul's inviolate door
To beat away the clang of hellish wings;
Who yet should be a lyre
Of high unquenchable desire
In the day of little things, —
Look where the amphoras,
The yield of many days,
Trod by my hot soul from the pulp of
    self,
And set upon the shelf
In sullen pride
The Vineyard-master's tasting to abide —
O mother mine!
Are these the bringings-in, the doings fine
Of him who used to praise?
Emptied and overthrown
The jars lie strown.

To Mother

These, for their flavor duly nursed,
Drip from the stopples vinegar accursed;
These, I thought honied to the very seal,
Dry, dry, — a little acid meal,
A pinch of mouldy dust,
Sole leavings of the amber-mantling must;
These rude to look upon,
But flasking up the liquor dearest won,
Through sacred hours and hard,
With watchings and with wrestlings and
     with grief,
Even of these, of these in chief,
The stale breath sickens reeking from the
     shard.
Nothing is left. Aye, how much less than
     naught!
What shall be said or thought
Of the slack hours and waste imaginings,
The cynic rending of the wings,
Known to the froward, that unreckoning
     heart
Whereof this brewage was the precious part,
Treasured and set away with furtive boast?
O dear and cruel ghost,
Be merciful, be just!
See, I was yours and I am in the dust.
Then look not so, as if all things were well!
Take your eyes from me, leave me to my
     shame,
Or else, if gaze they must,

The Young Mother

Steel them with judgment, darken them with
      blame;
But by the ways of light ineffable
You bade me go and I have faltered from,
By the low waters moaning out of hell
Whereto my feet have come,
Lay not on me these intolerable
Looks of rejoicing love, of pride, of happy
      trust!

Nothing dismayed?
By all I say and all I hint not made
Afraid?
O then, stay by me! Let
These eyes afflict me, cleanse me, keep me
      yet,
Brave eyes and true!
See how the shriveled heart, that long has
      lain
Dead to delight and pain,
Stirs, and begins again
To utter pleasant life, as if it knew
The wintry days were through;
As if in its awakening boughs it heard
The quick, sweet-spoken bird.
Strong eyes and brave,
Inexorable to save!

                William Vaughn Moody

To Mother

BABY'S SKIES

WOULD you know the baby's skies?
Baby's skies are mother's eyes.
Mother's eyes and smile together
Make the baby's pleasant weather.

Mother, keep your eyes from tears,
Keep your heart from foolish fears.
Keep your lips from dull complaining
Lest the baby think 't is raining.

M. C. Bartlett

THE MOTHER'S RETURN

A MONTH, sweet little ones, is past
Since your dear mother went away, —
And she to-morrow will return;
To-morrow is the happy day.

O blessed tidings! thought of joy!
The eldest heard with steady glee:
Silent he stood; then laughed amain, —
And shouted, " Mother, come to me!"

Louder and louder did he shout,
With witless hope to bring her near;
" Nay, patience! patience, little boy!
Your tender mother cannot hear."

16

The Young Mother

I told of hills, and far-off towns,
And long, long vales to travel through;
He listens, puzzled, sore perplexed,
But he submits; what can he do?

No strife disturbs his sister's breast;
She wars not with the Mystery
Of time and distance, night and day;
The bonds of our humanity,

Her joy is like an instinct, joy
Of kitten, bird, or summer fly;
She dances, runs without an aim,
She chatters in her ecstasy.

Her brother now takes up the note,
And answers back his sister's glee:
They hug the infant in my arms,
As if to force his sympathy.

Then, settling into fond discourse,
We rested in the garden bower;
While sweetly shone the evening sun
In his departing hour.

We told o'er all that we had done, —
Our rambles by the swift brook's side
Far as the willow-skirted pool,
Where two fair swans together glide.

To Mother

We talked of change, of winter gone,
Of green leaves on the hawthorn spray,
Of birds that build their nests and sing,
And all "since mother went away!"

To her these tales they will repeat,
To her our new-born tribes will show,
The goslings green, the ass's colt,
The lambs that in the meadow go.

But see, the evening star comes forth!
To bed the children must depart;
A moment's heaviness they feel,
A sadness at the heart:

'T is gone — and in a merry fit
They run up stairs in gamesome race;
I, too, infected by their mood,
I could have joined the wanton chase.

Five minutes past — and, O the change!
Asleep upon their beds they lie;
Their busy limbs in perfect rest,
And closed the sparkling eye.

Dorothy Wordsworth

SONG FROM "THE PRINCESS"

HOME they brought her warrior dead;
  She nor swoon'd nor utter'd cry.
All her maidens, watching, said,
  "She must weep or she will die."

The Young Mother

Then they praised him, soft and low,
   Call'd him worthy to be loved,
Truest friend and noblest foe;
   Yet she neither spoke nor moved.

Stole a maiden from her place,
   Lightly to the warrior stept,
Took the face-cloth from the face;
   Yet she neither moved nor wept.

Rose a nurse of ninety years,
   Set his child upon her knee —
Like summer tempest came her tears —
   " Sweet my child, I live for thee."
Alfred Tennyson

ALISON'S MOTHER TO THE BROOK

Brook, of the listening grass,
   Brook of the sun-fleckt wings,
   Brook of the same wild way and flicker-
      ing spell!
Must you begone? Will you forever
     pass,
After so many years and dear to tell? —
Brook of all hoverings . .
Brook that I kneel above;
Brook of my love.

19

To Mother

Ah, but I have a charm to trouble you;
A spell that shall subdue
Your all-escaping-heart, unheedful one
And unremembering!
Now, when I make my prayer
To your wild brightness there
That will but run and run,
O mindless Water! —
Hark, — now will I bring
A grace as wild, — my little yearling daugh-
      ter,
My Alison.

Heed well that threat;
And tremble for your hill-born liberty
So bright to see! —
Your shadow-dappled way, unthwarted yet,
And the high hills whence all your dearness
      bubbled; —
You, never to possess!
For let her dip but once — O fair and fleet, —
Here in your shallows, yes,
Here in your silverness
Her two blithe feet, —
O Brook of mine, how shall your heart be
      troubled!

The heart, the bright unmothering heart of
      you,
That never knew, —

The Young Mother

(O never, more than mine of long ago.
How could we know? —)
For who should guess
The shock and smiting of that perfect-
       ness? —
The lily-thrust of those ecstatic feet
Unpityingly sweet? —
Sweet beyond all the blurred blind dreams
       that grope
The upward paths of hope?
And who could guess
The dulcet holiness,
The lilt and gladness of those jocund feet,
Unpityingly sweet?
Ah, for your coolness that shall change and
       stir
With every glee of her! —
Under the fresh amaze
That drips and glistens from her wiles and
       ways;
When the endearing air
That everywhere
Must twine and fold and follow her, shall be
Rippled to ring on ring of melody, —
Music, like shadows from the joy of her,
Small starry Reveller! —
When from her triumphings, —
All frolic wings —
There soars beyond the glories of the height,
The laugh of her delight.

To Mother

And it shall sound, until
Your heart stand still;
Shaken to human sight;
Struck through with tears and light;
One with the one desire
Unto that central Fire
Of Love the Sun, whence all we lighted are
Even from clod to star.

And all your glory, O most swift and
      sweet! —
And all your exultation only this;
To be the lowly and forgotten kiss
Beneath those feet.

You that must ever pass, —
You of the same wild way, —
The silver-bright good-bye without a look! —
You that would never stay,
For the beseeching grass . . .
Brook! —

Josephine Preston Peabody

CHILDREN'S KISSES

So; it is nightfall then.
    The valley flush
    That beckoned home the way for herds
      and men,
Is hardly spent.

The Young Mother

Down the bright pathway winds, through
    veils of hush
And wonderment.
Unuttered yet, the chime
That tells of folding-time;
Hardly the sun has set.
The trees are sweetly troubled with bright
    words
From new-alighted birds; —
And yet, . . .
Here, — round my neck, are come to cling
    and twine,
The arms, the folding arms, close, close and
    fain,
All mine! —
I pleaded to, in vain,
I reached for, only to their dimpled scorning,
Down the blue halls of Morning;

Where all things else could lure them on
    and on,
Now here, now gone, —
From bush to bush, from beckoning bough
    to bough,
With bird-calls of *Come Hither!* —
                        . . . Ah, but now,
Now it is dusk. — And from his heaven of
    mirth,
A wilding skylark, sudden dropt to earth
Along the last low sunbeam yellow moted,

To Mother

Athrob with joy, —
There pushes here, a little golden Boy,
Still-gazing with great eyes.
And wonder-wise,
All fragrancy, all valor silver-throated,
My daughterling, my swan,
My Alison!

Closer than homing lambs against the bars
At folding-time, that crowd, all mother-
      warm,
They crowd, — they cling, they wreathe;
And thick as sparkles of the thronging stars,
Their kisses swarm.

O Rose of being, at whose heart I breathe,
Fold over; hold me fast
In the dark Eden of a blinding kiss.
And lightning heart's-desire, be still at last!
Heart can no more, —
Life can no more,
Than this.

Josephine Preston Peabody

MATERNAL GRIEF

DEPARTED CHILD! I could forget thee once
Though at my bosom nursed; this woeful
      gain
Thy dissolution brings, that in my soul

The Young Mother

Is present and perpetually abides
A shadow, never, never to be displaced
By the returning substance, seen or touched,
Seen by mine eyes, or clasped in my embrace.
Absence and death how differ they! and how
Shall I admit that nothing can restore
What one short sigh so easily removed? —
Death, life, and sleep, reality and thought,
Assist me, God, their boundaries to know,
O teach me calm submission to thy Will!
The Child she mourned had overstepped the
       pale
Of Infancy, but still did breathe the air
That sanctifies its confines, and partook
Reflected beams of that celestial light
To all the Little-ones on sinful earth
Not unvouchsafed — a light that warmed
      and cheered
Those several qualities of heart and mind
Which, in her own blest nature, rooted deep,
Daily before the Mother's watchful eye,
And not hers only, their peculiar charms
Unfolded, — beauty, for its present self,
And for its promises to future years,
With not unfrequent rapture fondly hailed.
Have you espied upon a dewy lawn
A pair of Leverets each provoking each
To a continuance of their fearless sport,
Two separate Creatures in their several gifts
Abounding, but so fashioned that, in all

That Nature prompts them to display, their
      looks,
Their starts of motion and their fits of rest,
An undistinguishable style appears
And character of gladness, as if Spring
Lodged in their innocent bosoms, and the
      spirit
Of rejoicing morning were their own?
Such union, in the lovely Girl maintained
And her twin Brother, had the parent seen,
Ere, pouncing like a ravenous bird of prey,
Death in a moment parted them, and left
The Mother, in her turns of anguish, worse
Than desolate; for oft-times from the sound
Of the survivor's sweetest voice (dear child,
He knew it not) and from his happiest
      looks,
Did she extract the food of self-reproach,
As one that lived ungrateful for the stay
By Heaven afforded to uphold her maimed
And tottering spirit. And full oft the Boy,
Now first acquainted with distress and grief,
Shrunk from his Mother's presence, shunned
      with fear
Her sad approach, and stole away to find,
In his known haunts of joy where'er he
      might,
A more congenial object. But, as time
Softened her pangs and reconciled the child
To what he saw, he gradually returned,

The Young Mother

Like a scared Bird encouraged to renew
A broken intercourse; and, while his eyes
Were yet with pensive fear and gentle awe
Turned upon her who bore him, she would
    stoop
To imprint a kiss that lacked not power to
    spread
Faint color over both their pallid cheeks,
And stilled his tremulous lip. Thus they
    were calmed
And cheered; and now together breathe
    fresh air
In open fields; and when the glare of day
Is gone, and twilight to the Mother's wish
Befriends the observance, readily they join
In walks whose boundary is the lost One's
    grave,
Which he with flowers had planted, finding
    there
Amusement, where the Mother does not
    miss
Dear consolation, kneeling on the turf
In prayer, yet blending with that solemn
    rite
Of pious faith the vanities of grief;
For such, by pitying Angels and by Spirits
Transferred to regions upon which the clouds
Of our weak nature rest not, must be deemed
Those willing tears, and unforbidden sighs,
And all those tokens of a cherished sorrow,

To Mother

Which, soothed and sweetened by the grace
    of Heaven
As now it is, seems to her own fond heart,
Immortal as the love that gave it being.
                        William Wordsworth

SONGS FOR MY MOTHER

I

HER HANDS

My mother's hands are cool and fair,
    They can do anything.
Delicate mercies hide them there
    Like flowers in the spring.

When I was small and could not sleep,
    She used to come to me,
And with my cheek upon her hand
    How sure my rest would be.

For everything she ever touched
    Of beautiful or fine,
Their memories living in her hands
    Would warm that sleep of mine.

Her hands remember how they played
    One time in meadow streams, —
And all the flickering song and shade
    Of water took my dreams.

28

The Young Mother

Swift through her haunted fingers pass
    Memories of garden things; —
I dipped my face in flowers and grass
    And sounds of hidden wings.

One time she touched the cloud that kissed
    Brown pastures bleak and far; —
I leaned my cheek into a mist
    And thought I was a star.

All this was very long ago
    And I am grown; but yet
The hand that lured my slumber so
    I never can forget.

For still when drowsiness comes on
    It seems so soft and cool,
Shaped happily beneath my cheek,
    Hollow and beautiful.

II

HER WORDS

My mother has the prettiest tricks
    Of words and words and words.
Her talk comes out as smooth and sleek
    As breasts of singing birds.

She shapes her speech all silver fine
    Because she loves it so.
And her own eyes begin to shine
    To hear her stories grow.

To Mother

And if she goes to make a call
   Or out to take a walk
We leave our work when she returns
   And run to hear her talk.

We had not dreamed these things were so
   Of sorrow and of mirth.
Her speech is as a thousand eyes
   Through which we see the earth.

God wove a web of loveliness,
   Of clouds and stars and birds,
But made not anything at all
   So beautiful as words.

They shine around our simple earth
   With golden shadowings,
And every common thing they touch
   Is exquisite with wings.

There's nothing poor and nothing small
   But is made fair with them.
They are the hands of living faith
   That touch the garment's hem.

They are as fair as bloom or air,
   They shine like any star,
And I am rich who learned from her
   How beautiful they are.
            Anna Hempstead Branch

MOTHERS of MEN

MOTHER AND POET

DEAD! One of them shot by the sea in the
   east,
   And one of them shot in the west by the
      sea.
Dead! both my boys! When you sit at the
   feast
   And are wanting a great song for Italy
      free,
   Let none look at *me!*

Yet I was a poetess only last year,
   And good at my art, for a woman men
      said;
But *this* woman, *this*, who is agoniz'd here,
   —The east sea and west sea rhyme on in
      her head
   Forever instead.

What art can a woman be good at? Oh, vain!
   What art *is* she good at, but hurting her
      breast
With the milk-teeth of babes, and a smile
   at the pain?
   Ah boys, how you hurt! you were strong
      as you pressed
   And I proud, by that test.

33

To Mother

What art's for a woman? To hold on
　　her knees
　　Both darlings; to feel all their arms
　　　round her throat,
Cling, strangle a little, to sew by de-
　　grees
　　And 'broider the long-clothes and neat
　　　little coat;
　　To dream and to doat.

To teach them. . . . It stings there! I
　　made them indeed
　　Speak plain the word *country*. I taught
　　　them, no doubt,
That a country's a thing men should die
　　for at need.
　　I prated of liberty, rights, and about
　　The tyrant cast out.

And when their eyes flashed . . . O my
　　beautiful eyes! . . .
　　I exulted; nay, let them go forth at the
　　　wheels
Of the guns, and denied not. But then
　　the surprise
　　When one sits quite alone! Then one
　　　weeps, then one kneels!
　　God, how the house feels!

At first, happy news came, in gay letters
    moil'd
  With my kisses,—of camp-life and glory,
    and how
They both lov'd me ; and, soon coming home
    to be spoil'd,
  In return would fan off every fly from my
    brow
  With their green laurel-bough.

Then was triumph at Turin : " Ancona was
    free ! "
  And some one came out of the cheers in
    the street,
With a face pale as stone, to say something
    to me.
  My Guido was dead ! I fell down at his
    feet,
  While they cheer'd in the street.

I bore it; friends sooth'd me ; my grief
    look'd sublime
  As the ransom of Italy. One boy re-
    main'd
To be leant on and walk'd with, recalling
    the time
  When the first grew immortal, while both
    of them strain'd
  To the height he had gain'd.

And letters still came, shorter, sadder, more
    strong,
    Writ now, but in one hand, " I was not
      to faint, —
One lov'd me for two — would be with me
    ere long:
    And *Viva l'Italia!* — *he* died for, **our**
      saint,
    Who forbids our complaint."

My Nanni would add, " he was safe, **and**
    aware
    Of a presence that turn'd off the balls, —
      was impress'd
It was Guido himself, who knew what I
    could bear,
    And how 't was impossible, quite dis-
      possess'd,
    To live on for the rest."

On which without pause, up the telegraph-
    line,
    Swept smoothly the next news from Gaeta:
      — *Shot.*
Tell his mother. Ah, ah, " his," "their "
    mother, — not " mine,"
    No voice says " *My* mother " again to me.
      What!
    You think Guido forgot?

Are souls straight so happy that, dizzy with
    Heaven,
  They drop earth's affections, conceive not
    of woe?
I think not. Themselves were too lately for-
    given
  Through that Love and Sorrow which rec-
    oncil'd so
  The Above and Below.

O Christ of the five wounds, who look'st
    through the dark
  To the face of Thy Mother! consider I
    pray,
How we common mothers stand desolate,
    mark,
  Whose sons, not being Christs, die with
    eyes turn'd away,
  And no last word to say!

Both boys dead? but that's out of nature.
    We all
  Have been patriots, yet each house must
    always keep one.
'T were imbecile, hewing out roads to a
    wall;
  And when Italy's made, for what end is
    it done
  If we have not a son?

Ah, ah, ah! when Gaeta's taken, what
    then?
  When the fair wicked queen sits no more
    at her sport
Of the fire-balls of death crashing souls out
    of men?
  When the guns of Cavilli with final re-
    tort
  Have cut the game short?

When Venice and Rome keep their own
    jubilee,
  When your flag takes all heaven for its
    white, green, and red,
When *you* have your country from mountain
    to sea,
  When King Victor has Italy's crown on
    his head,
  (And I have my Dead) —

What then? Do not mock me. Ah, ring
    your bells low,
  And burn your lights faintly! *My* country
    is *there*,
Above the star prick'd by the last peak of
    snow:
  My Italy's *there*, with my brave civic
    Pair,
  To disfranchise despair!

Forgive me. Some women bear children in
    strength,
  And bite back the cry of their pain in
    self-scorn;
But the birth-pangs of nations will wring us
    at length
  Into wail such as this — and we sit on
    forlorn
  When the man-child is born.

Dead! One of them shot by the sea in the
    east,
  And one of them shot in the west by the
    sea,
Both! both my boys! If in keeping the feast,
  You want a great song for your Italy free,
  Let none look at *me*.
           Elizabeth Barrett Browning

MOTHER WEPT

  Mother wept, and father sigh'd;
    With delight a-glow
  Cried the lad, " To-morrow," cried,
    "To the pit I go."

  Up and down the place he sped,
    Greeted old and young,
  Far and wide the tidings spread,
    Clapp'd his hands and sung.

To Mother

Came his cronies, some to gaze
   Rapt in wonder; some
Free with counsel; some with praise;
   Some with envy dumb.

" May he," many a gossip cried,
   " Be from peril kept ";
Father hid his face and sighed,
   Mother turned and wept.

Joseph Skipsey

HOW 'S MY BOY?

" Ho, Sailor of the sea!
   How 's my boy — my boy? "
" What 's your boy's name, good wife,
   And in what good ship sail'd he? "
" My boy John —
   He that went to sea —
   What care I for the ship, sailor?
   My boy 's my boy to me.

" You come back from sea,
   And not know my John?
   I might as well have ask'd some landsman
   Yonder down in the town.
   There 's not an ass in all the parish
   But he knows my John.

" How 's my boy — my boy?
   And unless you let me know

Mothers of Men

I 'll swear you are no sailor,
Blue jacket or no,
Brass buttons or no, sailor,
Anchor or crown or no!
Sure his ship was the Jolly Briton " —
" Speak low, woman, speak low ! "
" And why should I speak low, sailor,
About my own boy John?
If I was loud as I am proud
I'd sing him over the town!
Why should I speak low, sailor ? "
" That good ship went down."

" How 's my boy — my boy ?
What care I for the ship, sailor ?
I was never aboard her.
Be she afloat or be she aground,
Sinking or swimming, I 'll be bound,
Her owners can afford her !
I say how 's my John ? "
" Every man on board went down,
Every man aboard her."

" How 's my boy — my boy ?
What care I for the men, sailor ?
I 'm not their mother —
How 's my boy — my boy ?
Tell me of him and no other !
How 's my boy — my boy ? "

Sidney Dobell

To Mother

THE SAD MOTHER

O WHEN the half-light weaves
    Wild shadows on the floor,
How ghostly come the withered leaves
    Stealing about my door!

I sit and hold my breath,
    Lone in the lonely house;
Naught breaks the silence still as death,
    Only a creeping mouse.

The patter of leaves, it may be,
    But liker patter of feet,
The small feet of my own baby
    That never felt the heat.

The small feet of my son,
    Cold as the graveyard sod;
My little, dumb, unchristened one
    That may not win to God.

"Come in, dear babe," I cry,
    Opening the door so wide.
The leaves go stealing softly by;
    How dark it is outside!

And though I kneel and pray
    Long on the threshold-stone
The little feet press on their way,
    And I am ever alone.

Katharine Tynan Hinkson

Mothers of Men

LINES TO MY MOTHER'S PICTURE

O THAT those lips had language! Life has
        passed
With me but roughly since I heard thee last.
Those lips are thine, — thy own sweet smile
        I see,
The same that oft in childhood solaced me;
Voice only fails, else how distinct they say,
"Grieve not, my child; chase all thy fears
        away!"
The meek intelligence of those dear eyes
(Blest be the art that can immortalize,
The art that baffles time's tyrannic claim
To quench it!) here shines on me still the
        same.

   Faithful remembrance of one so dear,
O welcome guest, though unexpected here!
Who bid'st me honor with an artless song,
Affectionate, a mother lost long.
I will obey, not willingly alone,
But gladly, as the precept were her own;
And, while that face renews my filial grief,
Fancy shall weave a charm for my relief,
Shall steep me in Elysian revery,
A momentary dream that thou art she.

   My mother! when I learned that thou wast
        dead,
Say, wast thou conscious of the tears I shed?
Hovered thy spirit o'er thy sorrowing son,
Wretch even then, Life's journey just begun?
Perhaps thou gav'st me, though unfelt, a kiss;
Perhaps a tear, if souls can weep in bliss —
Ah, that smile! it answers — Yes.
I heard the bell tolled on thy burial day,
I saw the hearse that bore thee slow away,

And, turning from my nursery window, drew
A long, long sigh, and wept a last adieu.
But was it such? It was. Where thou art
    gone,
Adieus and farewells are a sound unknown.
May I but meet thee on that peaceful shore,
The parting words shall pass my lips no more!
Thy maidens, grieved themselves at my con-
    cern,
Oft gave me promise of thy quick return;
What ardently I wished I long believed,
And, disappointed still, was still deceived;
By expectation every day beguiled,
Dupe of to-morrow even from a child.
Thus many a sad to-morrow came and went,
Till, all my stock of infant sorrows spent,
I learned at last submission to my lot;
But, though I less deplored thee, ne'er for-
    got.
    Where once we dwelt our name is heard
    no more,
Children not thine have trod my nursery
    floor;
And where the gardener Robin, day by day,
Drew me to school along the public way,
Delighted with my bawble coach, and wrapped
In scarlet mantle warm, and velvet capped,
'T is now become a history little known,
That once we called the pastoral house our
    own.

Short-lived possession ! but the record fair,
That memory keeps of all thy kindness
    there,
Still outlives many a storm that has effaced
A thousand other themes less deeply traced.
Thy nightly visits to my chamber made,
That thou mightst know me safe and warmly
    laid, —
All this, and, more endearing still than all,
Thy constant flow of love, that knew no fall,
Ne'er roughened by those cataracts and
    breaks
That humor interposed too often makes, —
All this, still legible in memory's page,
And still to be so to my latest age,
Adds joy to duty, makes me glad to pay
Such honors to thee as my numbers may;
Perhaps a frail memorial, but sincere,
Not scorned in heaven, though little noticed
    here,
  Could Time, his flight reversed, restore
    the hours
When, playing with thy vesture's tissued
    flowers,
The violet, the pink, and jessamine,
I pricked them into paper with a pin,
(And thou wast happier than myself the
    while,
Wouldst softly speak, and stroke my head,
    and smile,) —

To Mother

Could those few pleasant days again appear,
Might one wish bring them, would I wish
    them here?
I would not trust my heart,— the dear de-
    light
Seems so to be desired, perhaps I might.
But no, — what here we call our life is such,
So little to be loved, and thou so much,
That I should ill requite thee to constrain,
Thy unbound spirit into bonds again.

    Thou, as a gallant bark from albion's
      coast
(The storms all weathered and the ocean
    crossed)
Shoots into port at some well-havened isle,
Where spices breathe and brighter seasons
    smile ;
There sits quiescent on the floods, that show
Her beauteous form reflected clear below,
While airs impregnated with incense play
Around her, fanning light her streamers
    gay, —
So thou, with sails how swift ! hast reached
    the shore,
Where tempests never beat, nor billows roar ;
And thy loved consort, on the dangerous tide
Of life, long since has anchored by thy side.
But me, scarce hoping to attain that rest,
Always from port withheld, always dis-
    tressed, —

Me howling blasts drive devious, tempest-
    tossed,
Sails ripped, seams opening wide, and com-
    pass lost;
And day by day some current's thwarting
    force
Sets me more distant from a prosperous
    course.
Yet O, the thought that thou art safe, and
    he! —
That thought is joy, arrive what may to me.
My boast is not that I deduce my birth
From loins enthroned, and rulers of the
    earth;
But higher far my proud pretensions rise, —
The son of parents passed into the skies.
And now farewell! — Time, unrevoked, has
    run
His wonted course, yet what I wished is
    done.
By contemplation's help, not sought in vain,
I seem to have lived my childhood o'er
    again, —
To have renewed the joys that once were mine
Without the sin of violating thine;
And while the wings of Fancy still are free,
And I can view this mimic show of thee,
Time has but half succeeded in his theft, —
Thyself removed, thy power to soothe me left.

                William Cowper

To Mother

MY MOTHER'S BIBLE

This book is all that's left me now, —
  Tears will unbidden start, —
With faltering lip and throbbing brow
  I press it to my heart.
For many generations past,
  Here is our family tree;
My mother's hands this Bible clasped,
  She, dying, gave it me.

Ah! well do I remember those
  Whose names these records bear;
Who round the hearthstone used to
      close,
  After the evening prayer,
And speak of what these pages said
  In tones my heart would thrill!
Though they are with the silent dead,
  Here are they living still!

My father read this holy book
  To brothers, sisters, dear;
How calm was my poor mother's look,
  Who loved God's word to hear!
Her angel face, — I see it yet!
  What thronging memories come!
Again that little group is met
  Within the halls of home!

Thou truest friend man ever knew,
   Thy constancy I 've tried;
When all were false, I found thee true,
   My counselor and guide.
The mines of earth no treasures give
   That could this volume buy;
In teaching me the way to live,
   It taught me how to die!
                  George Pope Morris

TWO SONS

I HAVE two sons, wife —
   Two and yet the same;
One his wild way runs, wife,
   Bringing us to shame.
The one is bearded, sunburnt, grim, and
      fights across the sea,
The other is a little child who sits upon your
      knee.

One is fierce and cold, wife,
   As the wayward deep;
Him no arms could hold, wife,
   Him no breast could keep.
He has tried our hearts for many a year, not
      broken them; for he
Is still the sinless little one that sits upon
      your knee.

51

To Mother

One may fall in fight, wife,
    Is he not our son?
Pray with all your might, wife,
    For the wayward one;
Pray for the dark, rough soldier, who fights
    across the sea,
Because you love the little shade who smiles
    upon your knee.

One across the foam, wife,
    As I speak may fall;
But this one at home, wife,
    Cannot die at all.
They both are only one; and how thankful
    should we be,
We cannot lose the darling son who sits upon
    your knee!

                  Robert Buchanan

MOTHER TO SON

BEFORE I knew the love of man
The lovely dream of you began.
When I said, " Jesus meek and mild,"
My Jesus was a little child.
I nursed the kitten on my knee,
And nursed you where no eye could see.
When I grew up to woman's grace
I saw you in your father's face,

Mothers of Men

Your hands were beating at my breast,
And gave my womanhood no rest,
Your little soul called each to each,
And laid bright heaven in our reach.
My body fed your body, son,
But birth 's a swift thing, swiftly done,
Compared to one-and-twenty years
Of feeding you with spirit's tears.
I could not make your mind and soul,
But my glad hands have kept you whole,
And tears have kept God's pastures green,
And washed the temple sweet and clean.
Think you that I have lived in vain
These years of wonder, joy, and pain?
The years when Jesus meek and mild
Was my beloved little child!
And when the first shy touch of things
Waked in my heart a thousand springs,
And bade me open childhood's gate
And give my woman's hand to fate!
The moment when your groping hands
Bound me to life with ruthless bands,
When all my living became a prayer,
And all my days built up a stair
For your young feet that trod behind,
That you an aspiring way should find!
Think you that life can give you pain,
Which does not stab in me again?
Think you that life can give you pleasure
Which is not my undying treasure?

To Mother

Think you that life can give you shame
Which does not make my pride go lame?
And you can do no evil thing
Which sears not me with poisoned sting.
Because of all that I have done,
Remember me in life, O son!
Keep that proud body fine and fair,
My love is monumented there.
For my love make no woman weep,
For my love hold no woman cheap,
And see you give no woman scorn
For that dark night when you were born.
     Beloved, all my years belong
     To you, go thread them for a song.
             Irene Rutherford McLeod

ONE MOTHER

MARY!
     I'm quite alone in all the world,
Into such bright sharp pain of anguish
     hurled
I cannot pray wise comfortable things;
Death's plunged me deep in hell, and given
     me wings
For terrible strange vastnesses; no hand
In all this empty spirit-driven space; I stand
Alone, and whimpering in my soul. I plod
Among wild stars, and hide my face from
     God.

God frightens me. He's strange. I know
    Him not.
And all my usual prayers I have forgot:
But you—you had a son—I remember now!
You are not Mary of the virgin brow!
You agonized for Jesus! You went down
Into the ugly depths for him. Your crown
Is my crown! I've seen you in the street,
Begging your way for broken bread and
    meat:
I've seen you in trams, in shops, among old
    faces,
Young eyes, brave lips, broad backs, in all
    the places
Where women work, and weep, in pain, in
    pride.
Your hands were gnarled that held him
    when he died!
Not the fair hands that painters give you,
    white
And slim. You never had such hands: night
And day you laboured, night and day, from
    child
To woman. You were never soft and mild,
But strong-limbed, patient, brown-skinned
    from the sun,
Deep-bosomed, brave-eyed, holy, holy One!
I know you now! I seek you, Mary! Spread
Your compassionate skirts! I bring to you
    my dead!

To Mother

This was my man. I bore him. I did not
  know
Then how he crowned me, but I felt it so.
He was my all the world. I loved him best
When he was helpless, clamouring at my
  breast.
Mothers are made like that. You'll under-
  stand
Who held your Jesus helpless in your hand
And loved his impotence. But as he grew
I watched him, always jealously, I knew
Each line of his young body, every tone
Of speech; his pains, his triumphs were my
  own.
I saw the down come on his cheeks with
  dread,
And soon I had to reach to hold his head
And stroke his mop of hair. I watched his eyes
When women crossed his ways, and I was
  wise
For him who had no wisdom. He was young,
And loathed my care, and lashed me with
  youth's tongue.
Splendidly merciless, casual of age, his scorn
Was sweet to me of whom his strength was
  born.
. . . Besides, when he was more than six
  foot tall
He kept the smile he had when he was
  small! . . .

And still no woman had him. I was glad
Of that — and then O God! The world ran
     mad!
Almost before I knew, this noise was war;
Death and not women took the son I bore . . .

You 'll know him when you see him: first of
     all
Because he 'll smile that way when he was
     small;
And then his eyes! They never changed
     from blue
To duller grey, as other children's do,
But like his childish dreams he kept his
     eyes
Vivid, and deeply clear, and vision wise.
Seek for him, Mary! Bright among the
     ghosts
Of other women's sons he 'll star those hosts
Of shining boys! (He always topped his
     class
At school!) Lean forward, Mary, as they
     pass,
And touch him! When you see his eyes
     you 'll weep
And think him your own Jesus! Let him
     sleep
In your deep bosom, Mary, then you 'll
     see
His lashes, how they curl, so childishly

To Mother

You'll weep again, and rock him on your
heart
As I did once, that night we had to part.
He'll come to you all bloody and be-mired,
But let him sleep, my dear, for he'll be tired,
And very shy. If he'd come home to me
I wouldn't ask the neighbours in to tea . . .
He always hated crowds . . . I'd let him
be. . . .

And then perhaps you'll take him by the
hand
And comfort him from fear when he must
stand
Before God's dreadful throne; then, will you
call
That boy whose bullet made my darling fall,
And take him by the other hand, and say . . .
" *O God, whose Son the hands of men did
slay,*
*These are Thy children who do take away
The sins of the world.* . . ."

Irene Rutherford McLeod

Mothers of Men

AN ENGLISH MOTHER [1]

EVERY week of every season out of English
    ports go forth,
White of sail or white of trail, East, or West,
    or South, or North,
Scattering like a flight of pigeons, half a
    hundred home-sick ships,
Bearing half a hundred striplings — each with
    kisses on his lips
Of some silent mother, fearful lest she shows
    herself too fond,
Giving him to bush or desert as one pays a
    sacred bond,
— Tell us, you who hide your heartbreak,
    which is sadder, when all 's done,
To repine an English mother, or to roam, an
    English son?

You who shared your babe's first sorrow when
    his cheek no longer pressed
On the perfect, snow-and-roseleaf beauty of
    your mother-breast,
In the rigor of his nurture was your woman's
    mercy mute,
Knowing he was doomed to exile with the
    savage and the brute?

To Mother

Did you school yourself to absence all his
    adolescent years,
That, though you be torn with parting, he
    should never see the tears?
Now his ship has left the offing for the many-
    mouthèd sea,
This your guerdon, empty heart, by empty
    bed to bend the knee?

And if he be but the latest thus to leave your
    dwindling board,
Is a sorrow less for being added to a sor-
    row's hoard?
Is the mother-pain duller that to-day his
    brothers stand,
Facing ambuscades of Congo, or alarms from
    Zululand?
Toil, where blizzards drift the snow like
    smoke across the plains of death?
Faint, where tropic fens at morning steam
    with fever-laden breath?
Die, that in some distant river's veins the
    English blood may run —
Mississippi, Yangtze, Ganges, Nile, Mac-
    kenzie, Amazon?

Ah! you still must wait and suffer in a soli-
    tude untold,
While your sisters of the nations call you
    passive, call you cold —

Still must scan the news of sailings, breath-
    less search the slow gazette,
Find the dreadful name . . . and, later, get
    his blithe farewell! And yet —
Shall the lonely hearthstone shame the legions
    who have died
Grudging not the price their country pays
    for progress and for pride?
— Nay; but, England, do not ask us thus to
    emulate your scars
Until women's tears are reckoned in the
    budgets of your wars.
              Robert Underwood Johnson

MATRES DOLOROSÆ

Ye Spartan mothers, gentle ones,
Of lion-hearted, loving sons
Fall'n, the flower of English youth,
To a barbarous foe in a land uncouth: —

O what a delicate sacrifice!
Unequal the stake and costly the price
As when the queen of Love deplor'd
Her darling by the wild beast gor'd.

They rode to war as if to the hunt,
But ye at home, ye bore the brunt,
Bore the siege of torturing fears,
Fed your hope on the bread of tears.

To Mother

Proud and spotless warriors they
With love or sword to lead the way;
For ye had cradled heart and hand,
The commander hearken'd to your com-
    mand.

Ah, weeping mothers, now all is o'er,
Ye know your honor and mourn no more:
Nor ask ye a name in England's story,
Who gave your dearest for her glory.
                  Robert Bridges

THE ABSENT SOLDIER SON

LORD, I am weeping. As Thou wilt, O Lord,
Do with him as Thou wilt; but O my God,
Let him come back to die! Let not the fowls
O' the air defile the body of my child,
My own fair child, that when he was a babe,
I lift up in my arms and gave to Thee!
Let not his garment, Lord, be vilely parted,
Nor the fine linen which these hands have
       spun
Fall to the stranger's lot! Shall the wild bird,
That would have pilfered of the ox, this year
Disdain the pens and stalls? Shall her blind
       young
That on the fleck and moult of brutish
       beasts
Had been too happy, sleep in cloth of gold

Whereof each thread is to this beating heart
As a peculiar darling? Lo, the flies
Hum o'er him! lo, a feather from the crow
Falls in his parted lips! Lo, his dead eyes
See not the raven! Lo, the worm, the worm,
Creeps from his festering corse? My God!
     my God!

.   .   .   .

O Lord, Thou doest well. I am content.
If Thou have need of him he shall not stay.
But as one calleth to a servant, saying
"At such a time be with me," so, O Lord,
Call him to Thee! O, bid him not in haste
Straight whence he standeth. Let him lay
     aside
The soiléd tools of labor. Let him wash
His hands of blood. Let him array himself
Meet for his Lord, pure from the sweat and
     fume
Of corporal travail! Lord, if he must die,
Let him die here. O, take him where Thou
     gavest!

                       Sidney Dobell

MOTHER AND SON

BRIGHTLY for him the future smiled,
   The world was all untried;
He had been a boy, almost a child,
   In your household till he died.

To Mother

And you saw him young and strong and fair
   But yesterday depart;
And you now know he is lying there
   Shot to death through the heart!

Alas, for the step so proud and true
   That struck on the war-path's track;
Alas, to go, as he went from you,
   And to come, as they brought him back!

One shining curl from that bright young head,
   Held sacred in your home,
Is all that you have to keep in his stead
   In the years that are to come.

You may claim of his beauty and his youth
   Only this little part —
It is not much with which to stanch
   The wound in a mother's heart!

It is not much with which to dry
   The bitter tears that flow;
Not much in your empty hands to lie
   As the seasons come and go.

Yet he has not lived and died in vain,
   For proudly you may say
He has left a name without a stain
   For your tears to wash away.

And evermore shall your life be blest,
  Though your treasures now are few,
Since you gave for your country's good the
    best
  God ever gave to you!

Phœbe Cary

MOTHERHOOD

MOTHER of Christ long slain, forth glided
    she,
  Following the children joyously astir
Under the cedars and the olive-tree,
  Pausing to let their laughter float to her.
Each voice an echo of a voice more dear,
  She saw a little Christ in every face.
When lo! another woman, passing near,
  Yearned o'er the tender life that filled the
    place,
And Mary sought the woman's hand, and
    said:
 "I know thee not, yet know thee memory-
    tossed
And what hath led thee here, as I am
    led—
  These bring to thee a child beloved and
    lost."

 "How radiant was my little one!
  And He was fair,

To Mother

Yea fairer than the fairest sun,
And like its rays through amber spun
   His sun-bright hair,
Still, I can see it shine and shine!"
  "Even so," the woman said, "was mine."

"His ways were ever darling ways,"
   And Mary smiled, —
"So soft and clinging! Glad relays
Of love were all his precious days —
   My little child
Was like an infinite that gleamed."
"Even so was mine," the woman dreamed.

Then whispered Mary: "Tell me, thou
   Of thine!" And she:
"Oh, mine was rosy as a bough
Blooming with roses, sent, somehow,
   To bloom for me!
His balmy fingers left a thrill
Within my breast that warms me still."

Then gazed she down some wilder, darker
     hour
And said, when Mary questioned knowing
     not:
"Who art thou, mother of so sweet a
     flower?"
"I am the mother of Iscariot."

Agnes Lee

CHRISTMAS
MOTHER POEMS

HYMN ON THE NATIVITY

It was the winter wild,
While the heaven-born child
   All meanly wrapt in the rude manger
      lies;
Nature, in awe of him,
Had doffed her gaudy trim,
   With her great Master so to sympathize:
It was no season then for her
To wanton with the sun, her lusty para-
      mour.

Only with speeches fair
She wooes the gentle air,
   To hide her guilty front with innocent
      snow;
And on her naked shame,
Pollute with sinful blame,
   The saintly veil of maiden-white to throw;
Confounded, that her Maker's eyes
Should look so near upon her foul deform-
      ities.

But he, her fears to cease,
Sent down the meek-eyed Peace:
   She, crowned with olive green, came softly
      sliding

To Mother

Down through the turning sphere,
His ready harbinger,
    With turtle wing the amorous clouds di-
        viding;
And, waving wide her myrtle wand,
She strikes a universal peace through sea
        and land.

No war or battle's sound
Was heard the world around:
    The idle spear and shield were high up-
        hung;
The hookèd chariot stood
Unstained with hostile blood;
    The trumpet spake not to the armèd
        throng;
And kings sat still with awful eye,
As if they surely knew their sovereign lord
        was by.

But peaceful was the night,
Wherein the Prince of Light
    His reign of peace upon the earth be-
        gan:
The winds, with wonder whist,
Smoothly the waters kissed,
    Whispering new joys to the mild ocean,
Who now hath quite forgot to rave,
While birds of calm sit brooding on the
        charmèd wave.

The stars, with deep amaze,
Stand fixed in steadfast gaze,
  Bending one way their precious influence;
And will not take their flight,
For all the morning light,
  Or Lucifer had often warned them thence;
But in their glimmering orbs did glow,
Until their Lord himself bespake, and bid
      them go.

And though the shady gloom
Had given day her room,
  The sun himself withheld his wonted speed,
And hid his head for shame,
As his inferior flame
  The new-enlightened world no more should
      need;
He saw a greater sun appear
Than his bright throne, or burning axle-
      tree, could bear.

The shepherds on the lawn,
Or ere the point of dawn,
  Sat simply chatting in a rustic row;
Full little thought they then
That the mighty Pan
  Was kindly come to live with them below;
Perhaps their loves, or else their sheep,
Was all that did their silly thoughts so busy
      keep.

To Mother

When such music sweet
Their hearts and ears did greet,
  As never was by mortal fingers strook,
Divinely warbled voice
Answering the stringèd noise,
  As all their souls in blissful rapture took:
The air, such pleasure loath to lose,
With thousand echoes still prolongs each
    heavenly close.

Nature, that heard such sound,
Beneath the hollow round
  Of Cynthia's seat, the airy region thrill-
    ing,
Now was almost won,
To think her part was done,
  And that her reign had here its last ful-
    filling;
She knew such harmony alone
Could hold all heaven and earth in happier
    union.

At last surrounds their sight
A globe of circular light,
  That with long beams the shame-faced
    night arrayed;
The helmèd cherubim,
And sworded seraphim,
  Are seen in glittering ranks with wings
    displayed,

Harping in loud and solemn quire,
With unexpressive notes, to Heaven's new-
    born heir.

Such music as 't is said
Before was never made,
  But when of old the sons of morning sung,
While the Creator great
His constellations set,
    And the well-balanced world on hinges
        hung,
And cast the dark foundations deep,
And bid the weltering waves their oozy chan-
    nel keep.

Ring out, ye crystal spheres,
Once bless our human ears,
  If ye have power to touch our senses so;
And let your silver chime
Move in melodious time;
    And let the bass of heaven's deep organ
        blow;
And, with your ninefold harmony,
Make up full concert to the angelic sym-
    phony.

For, if such holy song
Enwrap our fancy long,
  Time will run back, and fetch the age of
    gold;

And speckled Vanity
Will sicken soon and die,
   And leprous Sin will melt from earthly
      mould;
And Hell itself will pass away,
And leave her dolorous mansions to the peer-
      ing day.

Yea, Truth and Justice then
Will down return to men,
   Orbed in a rainbow; and, like glories
      wearing,
Mercy will sit between,
Throned in celestial sheen,
   With radiant feet the tissued clouds down
      steering;
And Heaven, as at some festival,
Will open wide the gates of her high palace
      hall.

But wisest Fate says no,
This must not yet be so;
   The babe yet lies in smiling infancy,
That on the bitter cross
Must redeem our loss,
   So both himself and us to glorify:
Yet first, to those ychained in sleep,
The wakeful trump of doom must thunder
      through the deep,

With such a horrid clang
As on Mount Sinai rang,
    While the red fire and smouldering clouds
        outbrake;
The aged earth aghast,
With terror of that blast,
    Shall from the surface to the center shake;
When, at the world's last session,
The dreadful Judge in middle air shall
        spread his throne.

And then at last our bliss,
Full and perfect is,
    But now begins; for, from this happy day,
The old dragon, under ground,
In straiter limits bound,
    Not half so far casts his usurpèd sway;
And, wroth to see his kingdom fail,
Swings the scaly horror of his folded tail.

The oracles are dumb;
No voice or hideous hum
    Runs through the archèd roof in words
        deceiving.
Apollo from his shrine
Can no more divine,
    With hollow shriek the steep of Delphos
        leaving.
No nightly trance, or breathèd spell,
Inspires the pale-eyed priest from the pro-
        phetic cell.

To Mother

The lonely mountains o'er,
And the resounding shore,
    A voice of weeping heard and loud lament;
From haunted spring and dale,
Edged with poplar pale,
    The parting Genius is with sighing sent;
With flower-inwoven tresses torn,
The nymphs in twilight shade of tangled
    thickets mourn.

In consecrated earth,
And on the holy hearth,
    The Lars and Lemures mourn with midnight plaint.
In urns and altars round,
A drear and dying sound
    Affrights the Flamens at their service
    quaint;
And the chill marble seems to sweat,
While each peculiar power foregoes his
    wonted seat.

Peor and Baälim
Forsake their temples dim
    With that twice-battered God of Palestine;
And moonèd Ashtaroth,
Heaven's queen and mother both,
    Now sits not girt with tapers' holy shine;

The Libyac Hammon shrinks his horn;
In vain the Tyrian maids their wounded
      Thammuz mourn.

And sullen Moloch, fled,
Hath left in shadows dread
  His burning idol all of blackest hue:
In vain with cymbals' ring
They call the grisly king,
  In dismal dance about the furnace
     blue:
The brutish gods of Nile as fast,
Isis, and Orus, and the dog Anubis, haste.

Nor is Osiris seen
In Memphian grove or green,
  Trampling the unshowered grass with
     lowings loud;
Nor can he be at rest
Within his sacred chest,
  Naught but profoundest hell can be his
     shroud;
In vain with timbreled anthems dark
The sable-stolèd sorcerers bear his wor-
     shiped ark.

He feels from Judah's land
The dreaded infant's hand,
  The rays of Bethlehem blind his dusky
     eyne;

Nor all the gods beside
Longer dare abide,
   Not Typhon huge ending in snaky twine;
Our babe, to show his Godhead true,
Can in his swaddling bands control the
     damnèd crew.

So, when the sun in bed,
Curtained with cloudy red,
   Pillows his chin upon an orient wave,
The flocking shadows pale
Troop to the infernal jail,
   Each fettered ghost slips to his several
     grave;
And the yellow-skirted fays
Fly after the night-steeds, leaving their
     moon-loved maze.

But see, the Virgin blest
Hath laid her babe to rest;
   Time is our tedious song should here have
     ending:
Heaven's youngest-teemèd star
Hath fixed her polished car,
   Her sleeping Lord with handmaid lamp
     attending;
And all about the courtly stable
Bright-harnessed angels sit in order serv-
     iceable.

                      John Milton

A MOTHER IN EGYPT

About midnight will I go out into the midst of Egypt:
and all the first-born in the land of Egypt shall die,
from the first-born of Pharaoh that sitteth upon his throne,
even unto the first-born of the maid-servant that is be-
hind the mill.

Is the noise of grief in the palace over the
    river
For this silent one at my side?
There came a hush in the night, and he rose
    with his hands a-quiver
Like lotus petals adrift on the swing of the
    tide.
O small cold hands, the day groweth old for
    sleeping!
O small still feet, rise up, for the hour is
    late!
Rise up, my son, for I hear them mourning
    and weeping
In the temple down by the gate!

Hushed is the face that was wont to brighten
    with laughter
When I sang at the mill;
And silence unbroken shall greet the sor-
    rowful dawns hereafter, —
The house shall be still.
Voice after voice takes up the burden of
    wailing —

79

To Mother

Do you not heed, do you not hear? — in the
    high priest's house by the wall.
But mine is the grief, and their sorrow is all
    unvailing.
Will he awake at their call?

Something I saw of the broad dim wings
    half folding
The passionless brow.
Something I saw of the sword that the shad-
    owy hands were holding, —
What matters it now?
I held you close, dear face, as I knelt and
    harkened
To the wind that cried last night like a soul
    in sin,
When the broad bright stars dropped down
    and the soft sky darkened
And the presence moved therein.

I have heard men speak in the market-place
    of the city,
Low-voiced, in a breath,
Of a God who is stronger than ours, and
    who knows not changing nor pity,
Whose anger is death.
Nothing I know of the lords of the outland
    races,

But Amud is gentle and Hathor the mother
    is mild,
And who would descend from the light of
    the Peaceful Places
To war on a child?

Yet here he lies, with a scarlet pomegranate
    petal
Blown down on his cheek.
The slow sun sinks to the sand like a shield
    of some burnished metal,
But he does not speak.
I have called, I have sung, but he neither
    will hear nor waken;
So lightly, so whitely, he lies in the curve
    of my arm,
Like a feather let fall from the bird the
    arrow hath taken, —
Who could see him, and harm?

"The swallow flies home to her sleep in the
    eaves of the altar,
And the crane to her nest." —
So do we sing o'er the mill, and why, ah,
    why should I falter,
Since he goes to his rest?
Does he play in their flowers as he played
    among these with his mother?

To Mother

Do the gods smile downward and love him
　　and give him their care?
Guard him well, O ye gods, till I come; lest
　　the wrath of that Other
Should reach to him there.

Marjorie L. C. Pickthall

CHRISTMAS CAROL

As Joseph was a-waukin',
　　He heard an angel sing,
"This night shall be the birthnight
　　Of Christ our heavenly King.

"His birth-bed shall be neither
　　In housen nor in hall,
Nor in the place of paradise,
　　But in the oxen's stall.

"He neither shall be rockèd
　　In silver nor in gold,
But in the wooden manger
　　That lieth in the mould.

"He neither shall be washen
　　With white wine nor with red,
But with the fair spring water
　　That on you shall be shed.

82

" He neither shall be clothèd
    In purple nor in pall,
But in the fair, white linen
    That usen babies all."

As Joseph was a-waukin',
    Thus did the angel sing,
And Mary's son at midnight
    Was born to be our King.

Then be you glad, good people,
    At this time of the year;
And light you up your candles,
    For His star it shineth clear.

                         Unknown

REGINA CŒLI

SAY, did his sisters wonder what could
       Joseph see
In a mild, silent little Maid like thee?
And was it awful in that narrow house,
With God for Babe and Spouse?
Nay, like thy simple, female sort, each
       one
Apt to find Him in Husband and in
       Son,
Nothing to thee came strange in this.
Thy wonder was but wondrous bliss:

To Mother

Wondrous, for, though
True Virgin lives not but does know,
(Howbeit none ever yet confess'd)
That God lies really in her breast,
Of thine He made His special nest
And so
All mothers worship little feet,
And kiss the very ground they 've trod;
But, ah, thy little Baby sweet
Who was indeed thy God!

Coventry Patmore

CHRIST THE MENDICANT

A STRANGER, to His own
He came; and one alone,
Who knew not sin,
His lowliness believed,
And in her soul conceived
To let Him in.

He naked was, and she
Of her humanity
A garment wove:
He hungered; and she gave,
What most His heart did crave,
A Mother's love.

John Banister Tabb

A CHRISTMAS CAROL

THERE 's a song in the air!
There 's a star in the sky!
There 's a mother's deep prayer
And a baby's low cry!
And the star rains its fire while the Beauti-
ful sing,
For the manger of Bethlehem cradles a king.

There 's a tumult of joy
O'er the wonderful birth,
For the virgin's sweet boy
Is the Lord of the earth.
Ay! the star rains its fire and the Beautiful
sing,
For the manger of Bethlehem cradles a king.

In the light of that star
Lie the ages impearled;
And that song from afar
Has swept over the world.
Every hearth is aflame, and the Beautiful sing
In the homes of the nations that Jesus is
King.

We rejoice in the light,
And we echo the song
That comes down through the night
From the heavenly throng.

To Mother

Ay! we shout to the lovely evangel they bring,
And we greet in his cradle our Saviour and
    King.

Josiah Gilbert Holland

A LITTLE CHILD'S HYMN

THOU that once, on mother's knee,
Wast a little one like me,
When I wake or go to bed
Lay thy hands about my head;
Let me feel thee very near,
Jesus Christ, our Saviour dear.

Be beside me in the light,
Close by me through all the night;
Make me gentle, kind, and true,
Do what mother bids me do;
Help and cheer me when I fret,
And forgive when I forget.

Once wast thou in cradle laid,
Baby bright in manger-shade,
With the oxen and the cows,
And the lambs outside the house:
Now thou art above the sky:
Canst thou hear a baby cry?

Thou art nearer when we pray,
Since thou art so far away;

Thou my little hymn wilt hear,
Jesus Christ, our Saviour dear,
Thou that once, on mother's knee,
Wast a little one like me.

Francis Turner Palgrave

A CAROL

HE came all so still
  Where His mother was,
As dew in April
  That falleth on the grass.

He came all so still
  Where His mother lay,
As dew in April
  That falleth on the spray.

He came all so still
  To His mother's bower,
As dew in April
  That falleth on the flower.

Mother and maiden
  Was never none but she!
Well might such a lady
  God's mother be.

Unknown.

LULLABIES

SEA SLUMBER–SONG

SEA-BIRDS are asleep,
The world forgets to weep,
Sea murmurs her soft slumber-song
On the shadowy sand
Of this elfin land;
" I, the Mother mild,
Hush thee, O my child,
Forget the voices wild!
Isles in elfin light
Dream, the rocks and caves,
Lull'd by whispering waves,
Veil their marbles bright,
Foam glimmers faintly white
Upon the shelly sand
Of this elfin land;
Sea-sound, like violins,
To slumber woos and wins,
I murmur my soft slumber-song,
Leave woes, and wails, and sins,
Ocean's shadowy night
Breathes good-night,
    Good-night!"

Roden Noel

To Mother

SWEET AND LOW

Sweet and low, sweet and low,
  Wind of the western sea,
Low, low, breathe and blow,
  Wind of the western sea!
Over the rolling waters go,
Come from the dying moon and blow,
  Blow him again to me;
While my little one, while my pretty one,
    sleeps.

Sleep and rest, sleep and rest,
  Father will come to thee soon;
Rest, rest, on mother's breast,
  Father will come to thee soon;
Father will come to his babe in the nest,
Silver sails all out of the west
  Under the silver moon;
Sleep, my little one, sleep, my pretty one,
    sleep.

Alfred Tennyson

A CRADLE HYMN

Hush! my dear, lie still and slumber,
  Holy angels guard thy bed!
Heavenly blessings without number
  Gently falling on thy head.

Lullabies

Sleep, my babe; thy food and raiment,
  House and home, thy friends provide;
All without thy care or payment:
  All thy wants are well supplied.

How much better thou 'rt attended
  Than the Son of God could be,
When from heaven He descended
  And became a child like thee!

Soft and easy is thy cradle:
  Coarse and hard thy Saviour lay,
When His birthplace was a stable
  And His softest bed was hay.

Blessèd babe! what glorious features —
  Spotless fair, divinely bright!
Must he dwell with brutal creatures?
  How could angels bear the sight?

Was there nothing but a manger
  Cursèd sinners could afford
To receive the heavenly stranger?
  Did they thus affront their Lord?

Soft, my child: I did not chide thee,
  Though my song might sound too hard;
'T is thy mother sits beside thee,
  And her arms shall be thy guard.

93

To Mother

Yet to read the shameful story
  How the men abused their King,
How they served the Lord of Glory,
  Makes me angry while I sing.

See the kinder shepherds round Him,
  Telling wonders from the sky!
Where they sought Him, there they found
      Him,
  With His Virgin mother by.

See the lovely babe a-dressing;
  Lovely infant, how He smiled!
When He wept, the mother's blessing
  Soothed and hushed the holy child.

Lo, He slumbers in His manger,
  Where the hornèd oxen fed;
Peace, my darling; here's no danger,
  Here's no ox anear thy bed.

'T was to save thee, child, from dying,
  Save my dear from burning flame,
Bitter groans and endless crying,
  That thy blest Redeemer came.

May'st thou live to know and fear Him,
  Trust and love Him all thy days;
Then go dwell forever near Him,
  See His face, and sing His praise.

Isaac Watts

CRADLE SONG

ERE the moon begins to rise
  Or a star to shine,
All the blue bells close their eyes —
  So close thine,
    Thine, dear, thine!

Birds are sleeping in the nest
  On the swaying bough,
Thus, against the mother-breast —
  So sleep thou,
    Sleep, sleep, thou!
        Thomas Bailey Aldrich

SLEEP, BABY, SLEEP

SLEEP, baby, sleep!
  Thy father watches the sheep;
Thy mother is shaking the dream-land tree,
And down falls a little dream on thee:
  Sleep, baby, sleep!

  Sleep, baby, sleep!
  The large stars are the sheep,
The little stars are the lambs I guess,
The fair moon is the shepherdess:
  Sleep, baby, sleep!
        Anonymous

To Mother

JAPANESE LULLABY

SLEEP, little pigeon, and fold your wings, —
   Little blue pigeon with velvet eyes;
Sleep to the singing of mother-bird swing-
      ing —
   Swinging the nest where her little one lies.

Away out yonder I see a star, —
   Silvery star with a tinkling song;
To the soft dew falling I hear it calling —
   Calling and tinkling the night along.

In through the window a moonbeam
      comes, —
   Little gold moonbeam with misty wings;
All silently creeping, it asks: " Is he sleep-
      ing —
   Sleeping and dreaming while mother
      sings? "

Up from the sea there floats the sob
   Of the waves that are breaking upon the
      shore,
As though they were groaning in anguish,
      and moaning —
   Bemoaning the ship that shall come no
      more.

But sleep, little pigeon, and fold your
  wings, —
  Little blue pigeon with mournful eyes;
Am I not singing? — see, I am swing-
  ing —
  Swinging the nest where my darling
  lies.

Eugene Field

THE COTTAGER'S LULLABY

THE days are cold, the nights are long;
The north-wind sings a doleful song;
Then hush again upon my breast,
All merry things are now at rest,
    Save thee, my pretty love!

The kitten sleeps upon the hearth,
The crickets long have ceased their mirth;
There's nothing stirring in the house
Save one wee, hungry, nibbling mouse;
    Then why so busy thou?

Nay, start not at that sparkling light;
'T is but the moon that shines so bright
On the window-pane bedropped with rain;
Then, little darling! sleep again,
    And wake when it is day.

Dorothy Wordsworth

To Mother

SWEDISH MOTHER'S LULLABY

THERE sitteth a dove, so fair and white,
 All on a lily spray;
And she listeneth how to the Saviour above
 The little children pray.

Lightly she spreads her friendly wings,
 And to heaven's gate hath sped,
And unto the Father in heaven she bears
 The prayers the children have said.

And back she comes from heaven's gate,
 And brings — that dove so mild —
From the Father in heaven, who hears her
  speak,
 A blessing for every child.

Frederika Bremer

THE ROAD TO SLUMBER–LAND

WHAT is the road to slumber-land and when
 does the baby go?
The road lies straight through mother's arms
 when the sun is sinking low.

He goes by the drowsy land of nod to the
 music of lullaby,
When all wee lambs are safe in the fold,
 under the evening sky.

Lullabies

A soft little nightgown clean and white; a
    face washed sweet and fair;
A mother brushing the tangles out of the
    silken, golden hair.

Two little tired, satiny feet, from shoe and
    stocking free;
Two little palms together clasped at the
    mother's patient knee.

Some baby words that are drowsily lisped to
    the tender Shepherd's ear;
And a kiss that only a mother can place on
    the brow of her baby dear.

A little round head that nestles at last close
    to the mother's breast,
And then the lullaby soft and low, singing
    the song of rest.

And closer and closer the blue-veined lids
    are hiding the baby eyes,
As over the road to slumber-land the dear
    little traveler hies.

For this is the way, through mother's arms,
    all little babies go
To the beautiful city of slumber-land when
    the sun is sinking low.

Mary Dow Brine

WYNKEN, BLYNKEN, AND NOD

WYNKEN, Blynken, and Nod one night
   Sailed off in a wooden shoe, —
Sailed on a river of crystal light
   Into a sea of dew.
"Where are you going, and what do you
      wish?"
   The old moon asked the three.
"We have come to fish for the herring fish
   That live in this beautiful sea;
   Nets of silver and gold have we!"
      Said Wynken,
      Blynken,
      And Nod.

The old moon laughed and sang a song,
   As they rocked in the wooden shoe;
And the wind that sped them all night
      long
   Ruffled the waves of dew.
The little stars were the herring fish
   That lived in that beautiful sea —
"Now cast your nets wherever you wish, —
   Never afeard are we!"
   So cried the stars to the fishermen three,
      Wynken,
      Blynken,
      And Nod.

All night long their nets they threw
　To the stars in the twinkling foam, —
Then down from the skies came the wooden
　　　shoe,
　Bringing the fishermen home :
'Twas all so pretty a sail, it seemed
　As if it could not be ;
And some folk thought 't was a dream they 'd
　　　dreamed
　Of sailing that beautiful sea ;
　But I shall name you the fishermen
　　　three :
　　　　Wynken,
　　　　Blynken,
　　　　And Nod.

Wynken and Blynken are two little eyes,
　And Nod is a little head
And the wooden shoe that sailed the skies
　Is a wee one's trundle-bed ;
So shut your eyes while Mother sings
　Of wonderful sights that be,
And you shall see the beautiful things
　As you rock in the misty sea
　Where the old shoe rocked the fishermen
　　　three : —
　　　　Wynken,
　　　　Blynken,
　　　　And Nod.

　　　　　　　　　　Eugene Field

To Mother

AULD DADDY DARKNESS

Auld Daddy Darkness creeps frae his hole,
Black as a blackamoor, blin' as a mole:
Stir the fire till it lowes, let the bairnie
    sit,
Auld Daddy Darkness is no want it yit.

See him in the corners hidin' frae the licht,
See him at the window gloomin' at the
    nicht;
Turn up the gas licht, close the shutters a',
An' Auld Daddy Darkness will flee far
    awa'.

Awa' to hide the birdie within its cosy nest,
Awa' to lap the wee flooers on their mither's
    breast,
Awa' to loosen Gaffer Toil frae his daily ca',
For Auld Daddy Darkness is kindly to a'.

He comes when we're weary to wean's frae
    oor waes,
He comes when the bairnies are getting off
    their claes ;
To cover them sae cosy, an' bring bonnie
    dreams,
So Auld Daddy Darkness is better than he
    seems.

102

Steek yer een, my wee tot, ye'll see Daddy
    then;
He's in below the bed claes, to cuddle ye
    he's fain;
Noo nestle to his bosie, sleep and dream yer
    fill,
Till Wee Davie Daylicht comes keekin' owre
    the hill.

                    James Ferguson

MOTHER–SONG

(From " Prince Lucifer ")

WHITE little hands!
   Pink little feet!
Dimpled all over,
   Sweet, sweet, sweet!
What dost thou wail for?
   The unknown? the unseen?
The ills that are coming,
   The joys that have been?

Cling to me closer,
   Closer and closer,
Till the pain that is purer
   Hath banished the grosser.
Drain, drain at the stream, love,
   Thy hunger is freeing,
That was born in a dream, love,
   Along with thy being!

To Mother

Little fingers that feel
　For their home on my breast,
Little lips that appeal
　For their nurture, their rest!
Why, why dost thou weep, dear?
　Nay, stifle thy cries,
Till the dew of thy sleep, dear,
　Lies soft on thine eyes.

Alfred Austin

SEPHESTIA'S LULLABY

(From " Menaphon ")

WEEP not, my wanton, smile upon my knee;
When thou art old there's grief enough for
　　thee.
　Mother's wag, pretty boy,
　Father's sorrow, father's joy;
　When thy father first did see
　Such a boy by him and me,
　He was glad, I was woe;
　Fortune changèd made him so,
　When he left his pretty boy,
　Last his sorrow, first his joy.

Weep not, my wanton, smile upon my knee;
When thou art old there's grief enough for
　　thee.
　Streaming tears that never stint,
　Like pearl-drops from a flint,

Fell by course from his eyes,
That one another's place supplies;
Thus he grieved in every part,
Tears of blood fell from his heart,
When he left his pretty boy,
Father's sorrow, father's joy.

Weep not, my wanton, smile upon my
    knee;
When thou art old there's grief enough for
    thee.
The wanton smiled, father wept,
Mother cried, baby leapt;
More he crowed, more we cried,
Nature could not sorrow hide:
He must go, he must kiss
Child and mother, baby bliss,
For he left his pretty boy,
Father's sorrow, father's joy.
Weep not, my wanton, smile upon my knee,
When thou art old there's grief enough for
    thee.

Robert Greene

CRADLE SONG

SLEEP, sleep, beauty bright,
Dreaming in the joys of night;
Sleep, sleep; in thy sleep
Little sorrows sit and weep.

To Mother

Sweet babe, in thy face
Soft desires I can trace,
Secret joys and secret smiles,
Little pretty infant wiles.

As thy softest limbs I feel
Smiles as of the morning steal
O'er thy cheek, and o'er thy breast
Where thy little heart doth rest.

O the cunning wiles that creep
In thy little heart asleep!
When thy little heart doth wake,
Then the dreadful night shall break.

William Blake

LULLABY OF AN INFANT CHIEF

O, HUSH thee, my babie, thy sire was a
     knight,
Thy mother a lady, both lovely and bright;
The woods and the glens, from the towers
     which we see,
They are all belonging, dear babie, to thee.
    O ho ro, i ri ri, cadul gu lo.

O, fear not the bugle, though loudly it
     blows,
It calls but the warders that guard thy re-
     pose;

Their bows would be bended, their blades
     would be red,
Ere the step of a foeman draws near to thy
     bed.
     O ho ro, i ri ri, cadul gu lo.

O, hush thee, my babie, the time soon will
     come,
When thy sleep shall be broken by trumpet
     and drum ;
Then hush thee, my darling, take rest while
     you may,
For strife comes with manhood, and waking
     with day.
     O ho ro, i ri ri, cadul gu lo.

                                   Walter Scott

The JOY of MOTHERHOOD

THE FIRSTBORN

So fair, so dear, so warm upon my bosom,
And in my hands the little rosy feet.
Sleep on, my little bird, my lamb, my blos-
    som ;
    Sleep on, sleep on, my sweet.

What is it God hath given me to cherish,
This living, moving wonder which is mine —
Mine only ? Leave it with me or I perish,
    Dear Lord of love divine.

Dear Lord, 't is wonderful beyond all won-
    der,
This tender miracle vouchsafed to me,
One with myself, yet just as far asunder
    That I myself may see.

Flesh of my flesh, and yet so subtly link-
    ing
New selfs with old, all things that I have
    been
With present joys beyond my former think-
    ing
    And future things unseen.

To Mother

There life began, and here it links with
heaven,
The golden chain of years scarce dipped
adown
From birth, ere once again a hold is given
And nearer to God's Throne.

Seen, held in arms and clasped around so
tightly, —
My love, my bird, I will not let thee go.
Yet soon the little rosy feet must lightly
Go pattering to and fro.

Mine, Lord, all mine Thy gift and loving
token.
Mine — yes or no, unseen its soul divine?
Mine by the chain of love with links un-
broken,
Dear Saviour, Thine and mine.

John Arthur Goodchild

BABY–LAND

" How many miles to Baby-Land?"
" Any one can tell;
Up one flight,
To the right;
Please to ring the bell."

The Joy of Motherhood

" What can you see in Baby-Land ? "
  " Little folks in white —
      Downy heads,
      Cradle-beds,
    Faces pure and bright ! "

" What do they do in Baby-Land ? "
  " Dream and wake and play,
      Laugh and crow,
      Shout and grow ;
    Jolly times have they ! "

" What do they say in Baby-Land ? "
  " Why, the oddest things ;
      Might as well
      Try to tell
    What a birdie sings ! "

" Who is the Queen of Baby-Land ? "
  " Mother, kind and sweet ;
      And her love,
      Born above,
    Guides the little feet."

George Cooper

MOTHER'S SONG

My heart is like a fountain true
That flows and flows with love to you.
As chirps the lark unto the tree
So chirps my pretty babe to me.
And it 's O ! sweet, sweet ! and a lullaby.

To Mother

There's not a rose where'er I seek,
As comely as my baby's cheek.
There's not a comb of honey-bee,
So full of sweets as babe to me.
And it's O! sweet, sweet! and a lullaby.

There's not a star that shines on high,
Is brighter than my baby's eye.
There's not a boat upon the sea,
Can dance as baby does to me.
And it's O! sweet, sweet! and a lullaby.

No silk was ever spun so fine
As is the hair of baby mine.
My baby smells more sweet to me
Than smells in spring the elder tree.
And it's O! sweet, sweet! and a lullaby.

A little fish swims in the well,
So in my heart does baby dwell.
A little flower blows on the tree,
My baby is the flower to me,
And it's O! sweet, sweet! and a lullaby.

The Queen has sceptre, crown and ball,
You are my sceptre, crown and all.
For all her robes of royal silk,
More fair your skin, as white as milk.
And it's O! sweet, sweet! and a lullaby.

114

The Joy of Motherhood

Ten thousand parks where deer do run,
Ten thousand roses in the sun,
Ten thousand pearls beneath the sea,
My babe more precious is to me.
And it's O! sweet, sweet! and a lullaby.

Unknown

CRADLE SONG

SLEEP, little baby of mine,
Night and the darkness are near,
But Jesus looks down
Through the shadows that frown,
And baby has nothing to fear.

Shut, little sleepy blue eyes;
Dear little head, be at rest;
Jesus, like you,
Was a baby once, too,
And slept on His own mother's
breast.

Sleep, little baby of mine,
Soft on your pillow so white;
Jesus is here
To watch over you, dear,
And nothing can harm you to-
night.

To Mother

O, little darling of mine,
What can you know of the bliss,
The comfort I keep,
Awake and asleep,
Because I am certain of this?

Unknown

CRADLE SONG

(From " Bitter-Sweet ")

WHAT is the little one thinking about?
Very wonderful things, no doubt!
    Unwritten history!
    Unfathomed mystery!
Yet he laughs and cries, and eats and drinks,
And chuckles and crows, and nods and
    winks,
As if his head were as full of kinks
And curious riddles as any sphinx!
  Warped by colic, and wet by tears,
  Punctured by pins, and tortured by fears,
  Our little nephew will lose two years;
    And he 'll never know
    Where the summers go; —
He need not laugh, for he 'll find it so!

Who can tell what a baby thinks?
Who can follow the gossamer links
  By which the mannikin feels his way

The Joy of Motherhood

Out from the shore of the great unknown,
Blind, and wailing, and alone,
  Into the light of day? —
Out from the shore of the unknown sea,
Tossing in pitiful agony; —
Of the unknown sea that reels and rolls,
Specked with the barks of little souls, —
Barks that were launched on the other side,
And slipped from Heaven on an ebbing
    tide!
  What does he think of his mother's eyes?
What does he think of his mother's hair?
  What of the cradle-roof that flies
Forward and backward through the air?
  What does he think of his mother's breast,
Bare and beautiful, smooth and white,
Seeking it ever with fresh delight, —
  Cup of his life, and couch of his rest?
What does he think when her quick embrace
Presses his hand and buries his face
Deep where the heart-throbs sink and swell
With a tenderness she can never tell,
  Though she murmur the words
  Of all the birds, —
Words she has learned to murmur well?
  Now he thinks he 'll go to sleep!
  I can see the shadow creep
  Over his eyes, in soft eclipse,
  Over his brow, and over his lips,
  Out to his little finger-tips!

To Mother

Softly sinking, down he goes!
Down he goes! down he goes!
See! he is hushed in sweet repose!
> *Josiah Gilbert Holland*

A SONG OF TWILIGHT

Oh, to come home once more, when the dusk
  is falling,
    To see the nursery lighted and the chil-
    dren's table spread;
"Mother, mother, mother!" the eager voices
  calling,
    "The baby was so sleepy that he had to go
    to bed!"

Oh, to come home once more, and see the
  smiling faces,
    Dark head, bright head, clustered at the
    pane;
Much the years have taken, when the heart
  its path retraces,
    But until time is not for me, the image
    will remain.

Men and women now they are, standing
  straight and steady,
    Grave heart, gay heart, fit for life's em-
    prise;

Shoulder set to shoulder, how should they be
 but ready!
  The future shines before them with the
  light of their own eyes.

Still each answers to my call; no good has
 been denied me,
  My burdens have been fitted to the little
  strength that's mine,
Beauty, pride and peace have walked by day
 beside me,
  The evening closes gently in, and how
  can I repine?

But oh, to see once more, when the early dusk
 is falling;
  The nursery windows glowing and the
  children's table spread;
"Mother, mother, mother!" the high child-
 voices calling,
  "He could n't stay awake for you, he had
  to go to bed!"

Unknown

TUCKING THE BABY IN

THE dark-fringed eyelids slowly close
  On eyes serene and deep;
Upon my breast my own sweet child
  Has gently dropped to sleep;

119

To Mother

I kiss his soft and dimpled cheek,
    I kiss his rounded chin,
Then lay him on his little bed,
    And tuck my baby in.

How fair and innocent he lies;
    Like some small angel strayed,
His face still warmed by God's own smile,
    That slumbers unafraid;
Or like some new embodied soul,
    Still pure from taint of sin —
My thoughts are reverent as I stoop
    To tuck my baby in.

What toil must stain these tiny hands
    That now lie still and white?
What shadows creep across the face
    That shines with morning light?
These wee pink shoeless feet — how far
    Shall go their lengthening tread,
When they no longer cuddled close
    May rest upon this bed?

O what am I that I should train
    An angel for the skies;
Or mix the potent draught that feeds
    The soul within these eyes?
I reach him up to the sinless Hands
    Before his cares begin, —
Great Father, with Thy folds of love,
    O tuck my baby in.

Curtis May

MOTHER AND CHILD

THE wind blew wide the casement, and
    within —
It was the loveliest picture ! — a sweet child
Lay in its mother's arms, and drew its life,
In pauses, from the fountain, — the white
    round
Part shaded by loose tresses, soft and dark,
Concealing, but still showing, the fair realm
Of so much rapture, as green shadowing
    trees
With beauty shroud the brooklet. The red
    lips
Were parted, and the cheek upon the breast
Lay close, and, like the young leaf of the
    flower,
Wore the same color, rich and warm and
    fresh : —
And such alone are beautiful. Its eye,
A full blue gem, most exquisitely set,
Looked archly on its world, — the little
    imp,
As if it knew even then that such a wreath
Were not for all ; and with its playful hands
It drew aside the robe that hid its realm,
And peeped and laughed aloud, and so it
    laid
Its head on the shrine of such pure joys,

And, laughing, slept. And while it slept, the
    tears
Of the sweet mother fell upon its cheek, —
Tears such as fall from April skies, and
    bring
The sunlight after. They were tears of joy;
And the true heart of that young mother
    then
Grew lighter, and she sang unconsciously
The silliest ballad-song that ever yet
Subdued the nursery's voices, and brought
    sleep
To fold her sabbath wings above its couch.
             William Gilmore Simms

MATERNITY

WITHIN the crib that stands beside my bed
    A little form in sweet abandon lies
    And as I bend above with misty eyes
I know how Mary's heart was comforted.

O world of Mothers! blest are we who know
    The ecstasy — the deep God-given
      thrill
    That Mary felt when all the earth was
      still
In the Judean starlight long ago!
             Anne P. L. Field

The Joy of Motherhood

MY BIRD

(Lines written at Burmah in joy for a first-born)

Ere last year's morn had left the sky,
  A birdling sought my Indian nest;
And folded, oh, so lovingly,
  Her tiny wings upon my breast.

From morning till evening's purple tinge,
  In winsome helplessness she lies;
Two rosy leaves with a silken fringe,
  Shut softly on her starry eyes.

There's not in Ind a lovelier bird;
  Broad earth owns not a happier nest;
O God, thou hast a fountain stirred,
  Whose waters never more shall rest.

This beautiful, mysterious thing,
  This seeming visitant from heaven,
This bird with the immortal wing,
  To me, to me, thy hand has given.

The pulse first caught its tiny stroke,
  The blood its crimson hue, from mine; —
This life which I have dared invoke,
  Henceforth, is parallel with thine.

A silent awe is in my room,
  I tremble with delicious fear;
The future, with its light and gloom,
  Time and eternity are here.

Doubts, hopes, in eager tumult rise,
  Hear, O my God, one earnest prayer:
Room for my bird in Paradise,
  And give her angel-plumage there.

Emily C. Judson

To Mother

CHILDREN

CHILDREN are what the mothers are.
No fondest father's fondest care
Can fashion so the infant heart
As those creative beams that dart,
With all their hopes and fears, upon
The cradle of a sleeping son.

His startled eyes with wonder see
A father near him on his knee,
Who wishes all the while to trace
The mother in his future face;
But 't is to her alone uprise
His waking arms; to her those eyes
Open with joy and not surprise.

Walter Savage Landor

MY LITTLE DEAR

MY little dear, so fast asleep,
   Whose arms about me cling,
What kisses shall she have to keep,
   While she is slumbering?

Upon her golden baby-hair,
   The golden dreams I'll kiss
Which Life spread through my
      morning fair,
   And I have saved, for this.

Upon her baby eyes I'll press
   The kiss Love gave to me,
When his great joy and loveliness
   Made all things fair to see.

126

And on her lips, with smiles astir,
   Ah me, what prayer of old
May now be kissed to comfort her,
   Should Love or Life grow cold.
                 Dollie Radford

THE IMMORTALITY OF LOVE

THEY sin who tell us love can die:
With life all other passions fly,
   All others are but vanity;
In heaven ambition cannot dwell,
Nor avarice in the vaults of hell;
Earthly these passions of the earth,
They perish where they have their
      birth;
   But love is indestructible;
Its holy flame for ever burneth,
From heaven it came, to heaven return-
      eth.
   Too oft on earth a troubled guest,
   At times deceived, at times op-
      press'd,
   It here is tried and purified,
   Then hath in heaven its perfect rest:
   It soweth here with toil and care,
   But the harvest-time of love is there.
Oh! when a mother meets on high
The babe she lost in infancy,

To Mother

Hath she not then, for pains and fears,
  The day of woe, the watchful night,
For all her sorrow, all her tears,
  An over-payment of delight?

                              Robert Southey

"THAT THEY ALL MAY BE ONE"

WHENE'ER there comes a little child,
My darling comes with him;
Whene'er I hear a birdie wild
Who sings his merry whim,
Mine sings with him:
If a low strain of music sails
Among melodious hills and dales,
When a white lamb or kitten leaps,
Or star, or vernal flower peeps,
When rainbow dews are pulsing joy,
Or sunny waves, or leaflets toy,
Then he who sleeps
Softly wakes within my heart;
With a kiss from him I start;
He lays his head upon my breast,
Tho' I may not see my guest,
Dear bosom-guest!
In all that's pure and fair and good,
I feel the spring-time of thy blood,
Hear thy whisper'd accents flow
To lighten woe,

The Joy of Motherhood

Feel them blend,
Although I fail to comprehend.
And if one woundeth with harsh word,
Or deed, a child, or beast, or bird,
It seems to strike weak Innocence
Through him, who hath for his defence
Thunder of the All-loving Sire,
And mine, to whom He gave the fire.
                              Roden Noel

OLD-FASHIONED MOTHER POEMS

MY MOTHER

WHO fed me from her gentle breast,
And hushed me in her arms to rest,
And on my cheek sweet kisses pressed?
                    My Mother.

When sleep forsook my open eye,
Who was it sang sweet lullaby,
And rocked me that I should not cry?
                    My Mother.

Who sat and watched my infant head,
When sleeping on my cradle bed,
And tears of sweet affection shed?
                    My Mother.

When pain and sickness made me cry,
Who gazed upon my heavy eye,
And wept for fear that I should die?
                    My Mother.

Who dressed my doll in clothes so gay,
And taught me pretty how to play,
And minded all I had to say?
                    My Mother.

To Mother

Who ran to help me when I fell,
And would some pretty story tell,
Or kiss the place to make it well?
                    My Mother.

Who taught my infant lips to pray,
And love God's holy book and day,
And walk in wisdom's Pleasant way?
                    My Mother.

And can I ever cease to be,
Affectionate and kind to thee,
Who was so very kind to me?
                    My Mother.

Ah! no, the thought I cannot bear,
And if God please my life to spare,
I hope I shall reward thy care,
                    My Mother.

When thou art feeble, old, and gray,
My healthy arms shall be thy stay,
And I will soothe thy pains away,
                    My Mother.

And when I see thee hang thy head,
'Twill be my turn to watch thy bed,
And tears of sweet affection shed,
                    My Mother.

For God, who lives above the skies,
Would look with vengeance in his eyes,
If I should ever dare despise
                    My Mother.
                              Jane Taylor

HALF–WAKING

I THOUGHT it was the little bed
    I slept in long ago;
A straight white curtain at the head,
    And two smooth knobs below.

I thought I saw the nursery fire,
    And in a chair well-known
My mother sat, and did not tire
    With reading all alone.

If I should make the slightest sound
    To show that I 'm awake,
She 'd rise, and lap the blankets round,
    My pillow softly shake;

Kiss me and turn my face to see
    The shadows on the wall,
And then sing " Rousseau's Dream " to
        me
    Till fast asleep I fall.

135

To Mother

But this is not my little bed;
 That time is far away:
With strangers now I live instead,
 From dreary day to day.

William Allingham

TO A CHILD EMBRACING HIS
MOTHER

LOVE thy mother, little one!
 Kiss and clasp her neck again —
Hereafter she may have a son
 Will kiss and clasp her neck in vain.
Love thy mother, little one!

Gaze upon her living eyes,
 And mirror back her love for thee, —
Hereafter thou mayst shudder sighs
 To meet them when they cannot see.
Gaze upon her living eyes!

Press her lips the while they glow
 With love that they have often told, —
Hereafter thou mayst press in woe,
 And kiss them till thine own are cold.
Press her lips the while they glow!

Oh, revere her raven hair!
 Although it be not silver-gray —

Too early Death, led on by Care,
   May snatch save one dear lock away.
Oh, revere her raven hair!

Pray for her at eve and morn,
   That Heaven may long the stroke defer; —
For thou mayst live the hour forlorn
   When thou wilt ask to die with her.
Pray for her at eve and morn!

Thomas Hood

WISHING

Ring-Ting! I wish I were a Primrose,
A bright yellow Primrose blowing in the
         spring!
   The stooping boughs above me,
   The wandering bee to love me,
   The fern and moss to creep across,
   And the Elm-tree for our king!

Nay — stay! I wish I were an Elm-tree,
A great lofty Elm-tree, with green leaves
         gay!
   The winds would set them dancing,
   The sun and moonshine glance in,
   The birds would house among the boughs,
   And sweetly sing!

To Mother

Oh — no! I wish I were a Robin.
A Robin or a little Wren, everywhere **to go;**
   Through forest, field or garden,
   And ask no leave or pardon,
   Till winter comes with icy thumbs
   To ruffle up our wing!

Well — tell! Where should I fly to,
Where go to sleep in the dark wood or dell?
   Before a day was over,
   Home comes the rover,
   For mother's kiss, — sweeter this
   Than any other thing!

William Allingham

THE VISIT

"Do you go to Norton, mamma, this next
   week?
I wish you had leisure to listen to me,
For when you are writing I don't like to
   speak,
   And that letter will never be finished, I
   see."

"I will lay down my pen, then, my dear little
   child,
   For I see you have minded the lesson we
   read;

138

Come, jump on my knee here," mamma said
and smiled,
  As she kissed the soft hair on her Emily's
  head.

" Yes, to Norton we are going, and what
shall I say
  To your two little playmates there, Har-
  riet and Ann?
Shall I say you can read now as well as can
play,
  And can pull out your needle as fast as
  they can?"

" No, mamma, that was not what I wished
you to hear!
  And I fear you won't like what I'm going
  to say;
Stop, put down your head, let me speak in
your ear,
  For to whisper, I think, is by much the
  best way."

She asked to be taken her young friends to
see,
  And to show them her work-box, her dolls,
  and her toys;
She said she would try such a good child to be,
  And be well-bred and kind to the two
  little boys.

139

She said if they teased her, or for her dolls
cried,
　　She would not forget she was older than
　　they,
If as boys they were rude, she would try
not to chide,
　　But would put up the dolls until they
　　went away.

From Ann she could learn how her bracelets
to string,
　　And with Harriet would practice doll's
　　bonnets to make;
She would give to the latter her favorite
ring,
　　And for dear little Ann, that Dutch doll
　　she would take.

"Then pray, dear mamma, pray do not say
no;
　　You are always so kind, do indulge me in
　　this:
I think if you like it, papa'll let me go,
　　And I shall be so good, I'll do nothing
　　amiss."

Papa was consulted, and though it was
far,
　　Little Emily's goodness and worth gained
　　the day,

She was promised to go when the next week
    came round,
    And see — there is the carriage now driv-
    ing away.
                        Rhymes for the Nursery

THE BABY

WHAT is the pretty little thing
That nurse so carefully doth bring,
And round its head her apron fling?
                    A baby.

Oh, dear, how very soft its cheek:
Why, nurse, I cannot make it speak,
And it can't walk, it is so weak,
                    Poor baby.

Here take a bite, you little dear,
I 've got some cake and sweetmeats here,
'T is very nice, you need not fear,
                    You baby.

Oh, I 'm afraid that it will die,
Why can't it eat as well as I,
And jump, and talk? do let it try,
                    Poor baby.

Why, you were once a baby too,
And could not jump, as now you do,
But good mamma took care of you,
                    Like baby.

To Mother

And then she taught your pretty feet
To pat along the carpet neat,
And called papa to come and meet
    His baby.

Oh, good mamma, to take such care,
And no kind pains and trouble spare,
To feed and nurse you when you were
    A baby.
     Jane and Ann Taylor

GETTING UP

BABY, baby, ope your eye,
For the sun is in the sky,
And he 's peeping once again
Through the frosty window pane;
Little baby, do not keep
Any longer fast asleep.

There, now, sit in mother's lap,
That she may untie your cap,
For the little strings have got
Twisted into such a knot;
Ah! for shame, — you 've been at play
With the bobbin, as you lay.

There it comes, — now let me see
Where your petticoats can be;

Oh, — they 're in the window seat,
Folded very smooth and neat:
When my baby older grows
She shall double up her clothes.

Now one pretty little kiss,
For dressing you as neat as this,
And before we go downstairs,
Don't forget to say your pray'rs,
For 't is God who loves to keep
Little babies in their sleep.

Jane Taylor

MAMMA!

(From "The Floweret")

MY own mamma!
My dear mamma!
How happy I shall be,
To-morrow night,
At candle-light,
When she comes home to me.

To-morrow night,
At candle-light, —
Yes, that 's the time, they say,
That she 'll be here,
Our mother dear, —
How long she 's been away.

To Mother

'T is just a week,
Since on my cheek
She pressed the parting kiss;
It seems like two, —
I never knew
So long a week as this.

My tangled hair
She smoothed with care,
With water bathed my brow;
And all with such
A gentle touch, —
There 's none to do so now.

I cannot play
When she 's away;
There 's none to laugh with me;
And much I miss
The tender kiss, —
The seat upon her knee.

When up to bed
I 'm sorrowing led,
I linger on the stairs;
I lie and weep —
I cannot sleep —
I scarce can say my prayers.

But she will come,
She 'll be at home
To-morrow night, and then
I hope that she
Will never be
So long away again.

Anna M. Wells

TO MY MOTHER

THEY tell us of an Indian tree
  Which howsoe'er the sun and sky
May tempt its boughs to wander free,
  And shoot and blossom, wide and high,
Far better loves to bend its arms
  Downward again to that dear earth
From which the life, that fills and warms
  Its grateful being, first had birth.
'T is thus, though wooed by flattering friends,
  And fed with fame (if fame it be),
This heart, my own dear mother, bends,
  With love's true instinct, back to thee!

Thomas Moore

CUDDLE DOON

THE bairnies cuddle doon at nicht
  Wi' muckle faught an' din;
" Oh try and sleep, ye waukrife rogues,
  Your faither 's comin' in."

145

To Mother

They never heed a word I speak;
   I try to gie a froon,
But aye I hap them up an' cry,
   "Oh, bairnies, cuddle doon."

Wee Jamie wi' the curly heid —
   He aye sleeps next the wa' —
Bangs up an' cries, " I want a piece;"
   The rascal starts them a'.
I rin and fetch them pieces, drinks,
   They stop awee the soun',
Then draw the blankets up an' cry,
   " Noo, weanies, cuddle doon."

But, ere five minutes gang, wee Rab
   Cries out, frae 'neath the claes,
" Mither, mak' Tam gie ower at ance,
   He 's kittlin' wi' his taes."
The mischief 's in that Tam for tricks,
   He 'd bother half the toon;
But aye I hap them up and cry,
   " Oh, bairnies, cuddle doon."

At length they hear their father's fit,
   An', as he steeks the door,
They turn their faces to the wa',
   While Tam pretends to snore.
" Hae a' the weans been gude?" he asks,
   As he pits aff his shoon;
" The bairnies, John, are in their beds,
   An' lang since cuddled doon."

An' just afore we bed oorsels,
  We look at our wee lambs;
Tam has his airm roun' wee Rab's
    neck,
  And Rab his airm round Tam's.
I lift wee Jamie up the bed,
  An' as I straik each croon,
I whisper, till my heart fills up,
 "Oh, bairnies, cuddle doon."

The bairnies cuddle doon at nicht
  Wi' mirth that 's dear to me;
But soon the big warl's cark an' care
  Will quaten doon their glee.
Yet, come what will to ilka ane,
  May He who rules aboon
Aye whisper, though their pows be
    bald,
 "Oh, bairnies, cuddle doon."
                    Alexander Anderson

THE BABY

Safe sleeping on its mother's breast
  The smiling babe appears,
Now sweetly sinking into rest;
  Now washed in sudden tears:
Hush, hush, my little baby dear,
There 's nobody to hurt you here.

To Mother

Without a mother's tender care,
   The little thing must die,
Its chubby hands too feeble are
   One service to supply;
And not a tittle does it know
What kind of world 't is come into.

The lambs sport gayly on the grass
   When scarcely born a day;
The foal, beside its mother ass,
   Trots frolicksome away,
No other creature, tame or wild,
Is half so helpless as a child.

To nurse the Dolly, gayly drest,
   And stroke its flaxen hair,
Or ring the coral at its waist,
   With silver bells so fair,
Is all the little creature can,
That is so soon to be a man.

Full many a summer's sun must glow
   And lighten up the skies,
Before its tender limbs can grow
   To anything of size;
And all the while the mother's eye
Must every little want supply.

Then surely, when each little limb
   Shall grow to healthy size,

And youth and manhood strengthen him
  For toil and enterprise,
His mother's kindness is a debt,
He never, never will forget.

Jane Taylor

GOOD–NIGHT

LITTLE baby, lay your head
On your pretty cradle-bed;
Shut your eye-peeps now the day
And the light are gone away;
All the clothes are tucked in tight;
Little baby dear, good-night.

Yes, my darling, well I know
How the bitter wind doth blow;
And the winter's snow and rain
Patter on the window-pane:
But they cannot come in here,
To my little baby dear;

For the window shutteth fast,
Till the stormy night is past;
And the curtains warm are spread
Round about her cradle bed:
So till morning shineth bright
Little baby dear, good-night.

Jane Taylor

THE OLD ARM–CHAIR

I LOVE it! I love it! and who shall dare
To chide me for loving that old arm-chair?
I 've treasured it long as a sainted prize,
I 've bedew'd it with tears, and embalm'd it
        with sighs;
'T is bound by a thousand bands to my heart;
Not a tie will break, not a link will start.
Would ye learn the spell?— a mother sat
        there,
And a sacred thing is that old arm-chair.

In childhood's hour I linger'd near
The hallow'd seat with listening ear;
And gentle words that mother would give,
To fit me to die and teach me to live:
She told me shame would never betide
With truth for my creed and God for my
        guide;
She taught me to lisp my earliest prayer,
As I knelt beside that old arm-chair.

I sat and watch'd her many a day,
When her eye grew dim, and her locks were
        gray;
And I almost worshipp'd her when she
        smiled,
And turn'd from her Bible to bless her child.

Old-Fashioned Mother Poems

Years roll'd on, but the last one sped —
My idol was shatter'd, my earth-star fled;
I learnt how much the heart can bear,
When I saw her die in that old arm-chair.

'T is past! 't is past! but I gaze on it now
With quivering breath and throbbing brow:
'T was there she nursed me, 't was there she
     died;
And memory flows with lava tide.
Say it is folly, and deem me weak,
While the scalding drops start down my
     cheek;
But I love, I love it! and cannot tear
My soul from a mother's old arm-chair.

Eliza Cook

SONNETS on MOTHERHOOD

AD MATREM

OFT in the after days, when thou and I
Have fallen from the cope of human view,
When, both together, under the sweet sky
We sleep beneath the daisies and the dew,
Men will recall thy gracious presence bland,
Conning the pictured sweetness of thy face;
Will pore o'er paintings by thy plastic hand,
And vaunt thy skill, and tell thy deeds of
      grace.
Oh may they then, who crown thee with true
      bays,
Saying, " What love unto her son she bore ! "
Make this addition to thy perfect praise,
" Nor ever yet was mother worshiped
      more ! "
So shall I live with thee, and thy dear fame
Shall link my love unto thine honored name.
                    Julian Henry Fane

NATURE

AS a fond mother, when the day is o'er,
   Leads by the hand her little child to bed,
   Half willing, half reluctant to be led,
   And leave his broken playthings on the
      floor,

To Mother

Still gazing at them through the open door,
   Nor wholly reassured and comforted
   By promises of others in their stead,
   Which, though more splendid, may not
      please him more ;
So Nature deals with us, and takes away
   Our playthings one by one, and by the
      hand
   Leads us to rest so gently, that we go
Scarce knowing if we wish to go or stay,
   Being too full of sleep to understand
   How far the unknown transcends the what
      we know.

Henry Wadsworth Longfellow

BEDTIME

'T is bedtime ; say your hymn, and bid
   " Good-night ;
God bless Mamma, Papa, and dear ones
   all."
Your half-shut eyes beneath your eyelids
   fall,
Another minute, you will shut them quite.
Yes, I will carry you, put out the light,
And tuck you up, although you are so
   tall !
What will you give me, sleepy one, and call
My wages, if I settle you all right?
I laid her golden curls upon my arm,

156

I drew her little feet within my hand,
Her rosy palms were joined in trustful bliss,
Her heart next mine beat gently, soft and
    warm
She nestled to me, by Love's command,
Paid me my precious wages — "Baby's
    Kiss."

Francis, Earl of Rosslyn

HER FIRSTBORN

It was her first sweet child, her heart's de-
    light:
And, though we all foresaw his early doom,
We kept the fearful secret out of sight;
We saw the canker, but she kiss'd the bloom.
And yet it might not be: we could not
    brook
To vex her happy heart with vague alarms,
To blanch with fear her fond intrepid look,
Or send a thrill through those encircling
    arms.
She smil'd upon him, waking or at rest:
She could not dream her little child would
    die:
She toss'd him fondly with an upward eye:
She seem'd as buoyant as a summer spray,
That dances with a blossom on its breast,
Nor knows how soon it will be borne away.

Charles Tennyson Turner

TO A YOUNG CHILD

As doth his heart who travels far from home
Leap up whenever he by chance doth see
One from his mother-country lately come,
Friend from my home — thus do I welcome
    thee.
Thou art so late arrived that I the tale
Of thy high lineage on thy brow can trace,
And almost feel the breath of that soft gale
That wafted thee unto this desert place,
And half can hear those ravishing sounds
    that flowed
From out Heaven's gate when it was oped
    for thee,
That thou awhile mightst leave thy bright
    abode
Amid these lone and desolate tracks to be
A homesick, weary wanderer, and then
Return unto thy native land again.

               Eliza Scudder

THE VIRGIN

MOTHER! whose virgin bosom was uncrost
With the least shade of thought to sin allied;
Woman! above all women glorified,
Our tainted nature's solitary boast;
Purer than foam on central ocean tost;

Brighter than eastern skies at daybreak
    strewn
With fancied roses, than the unblemished
    moon
Before her wane begins on heaven's blue
    coast ;
Thy image falls to earth. Yet some, I ween,
Not unforgiven the suppliant knee might
    bend,
As to a visible Power, in which did blend
All that was mixed and reconciled in Thee
Of mother's love with maiden purity,
Of high with low, celestial with terrene !

William Wordsworth

THANKSGIVING AFTER CHILDBIRTH

WOMAN! the Power who left his throne on
    high,
And deigned to wear the robe of flesh we
    wear,
The Power that thro' the straits of Infancy
Did pass dependent on maternal care,
His own humanity with Thee will share,
Pleased with the thanks that in his People's
    eye
Thou offerest up for safe Delivery
From Childbirth's perilous throes. And
    should the Heir

To Mother

Of thy fond hopes hereafter walk inclined
To courses fit to make a mother rue
That ever he was born, a glance of mind
Cast upon this observance may renew
A better will; and, in the imagined view
Of thee thus kneeling, safety he may find.
William Wordsworth

MY MOTHER

THERE was a gather'd stillness in the room:
Only the breathing of the great sea rose
From far off, aiding that profound repose,
With regular pulse and pause within the
gloom
Of twilight, as if some impending doom
Was now approaching;— I sat moveless there,
Watching with tears and thoughts that were
like prayer,
Till the hour struck,— the thread dropp'd
from the loom;
And the Bark pass'd in which freed souls
are borne.
The dear still'd face lay there; that sound
forlorn
Continued; I rose not, but long sat by:
And now my heart oft hears that sad seashore,
When she is in the far-off land, and I
Wait the dark sail returning yet once more.
William Bell Scott

160

EVENING

AGE cannot wither her whom not gray hairs
Nor furrowed cheeks have made the thrall
    of Time;
For Spring lies hidden under Winter's rime,
And violets know the victory is theirs.
Even so the corn of Egypt, unawares,
Proud Nilus shelters with engulfing slime;
So Etna's hardening crust a more sublime
Volley of pent-up fires at last prepares.
O face yet fair, if paler, and serene
With sense of duty done without complaint!
O venerable crown! — a living green,
Strength to the weak, and courage to the
    faint —
Thy bleaching locks, thy wrinkles, have but
    been
Fresh beads upon the rosary of a saint!
            Wendell Phillips Garrison

TO MY FIRST LOVE, MY MOTHER

SONNETS are full of love, and this my tome
   Has many sonnets: so here now shall be
   One sonnet more, a love sonnet, from me
To her whose heart is my heart's quiet home,
   To my first Love, my Mother, on whose
   knee

To Mother

I learnt love-lore that is not troublesome;
  Whose service is my special dignity,
And she my lodestar while I go and come.

And so because you love me, and because
    I love you, Mother, I have woven a
        wreath
      Of rhymes wherewith to crown your
        honored name:
      In you not fourscore years can dim the
        flame
Of love, whose blessed glow transcends the
        laws
    Of time and change and mortal life and
        death.

Christina G. Rossetti

TRIBUTES to MOTHERS

MOTHER O' MINE[1]

IF I were hanged on the highest hill,
   Mother o' mine, O mother o' mine!
I know whose love would follow me still,
   Mother o' mine, O mother o' mine!

If I were drowned in the deepest sea,
   Mother o' mine, O mother o' mine!
I know whose tears would come down to me,
   Mother o' mine, O mother o' mine!

If I were damned of body and soul,
I know whose prayers would make me whole,
   Mother o' mine, O mother o' mine!
              Rudyard Kipling

AT BETHLEHEM

LONG, long before the Babe could speak,
When he would kiss his mother's cheek
   And to her bosom press,
The brightest angels standing near
Would turn away to hide a tear —
   For they are motherless.

[1] By permission of the author, Rudyard Kipling. From *The Light that Failed*, copyright, 1899, by Rudyard Kipling.

165

To Mother

Where were ye, Birds, that bless His name,
When wingless to the world He came,
And wordless, though Himself the Word
That made the blossom and the bird?

John Banister Tabb

TO HIS MOTHER

He brought a Lily white,
That bowed its fragrant head
And blushed a rosy red.
Before her fairer light.

He brought a rose; and, lo,
The crimson blossom saw
Her beauty, and in awe
Became as white as snow.

John Banister Tabb

THE SHEPHERDESS

She walks — the lady of my delight —
    A shepherdess of sheep.
Her flocks are thoughts. She keeps them
        white;
    She guards them from the steep.
She feeds them on the fragrant height,
    And folds them in for sleep.

She roams maternal hills and bright,
    Dark valleys safe and deep.
Into that tender breast at night
    The chastest stars may peep.
She walks — the lady of my delight —
    A shepherdess of sheep.

She holds her little thoughts in sight,
    Though gay they run and leap.
She is so circumspect and right;
    She has her soul to keep.
She walks — the lady of my delight —
    A shepherdess of sheep.

              Alice Meynell

MOTHERLESS

I WRITE. My mother was a Florentine,
Whose rare blue eyes were shut from seeing
    me
When scarcely I was four years old ; my life,
A poor spark snatched up from a failing lamp
Which went out therefore. She was weak
    and frail;
She could not bear the joy of giving life —
The mother's rapture slew her. If her kiss
Had left a longer weight upon my lips,
It might have steadied the uneasy breath,
And reconciled and fraternized my soul
With a new order. As it was, indeed,

To Mother

I felt a mother-want about the world,
And still went seeking, like a bleating lamb
Left out at night, in shutting up the fold, —
As restless as a nest-deserted bird
Grown chill through something being away,
      though what
It knows not. I, Aurora Leigh, was born
To make my father sadder, and myself
Not overjoyous, truly. Women know
The way to rear up children (to be just)
They know a simple, merry, tender knack
Of tying sashes, fitting baby-shoes,
And stringing pretty words that make no
      sense,
And kissing full sense into empty words;
Which things are corals to cut life upon,
Although such trifles: children learn by such
Love's holy earnest in a pretty play,
And get not over-early solemnized, —
But seeing, as in a rose-bush, Love's Divine,
Which burns and hurts not, — not a single
      bloom, —
Become aware and unafraid of Love.
Such good do mothers. Fathers love as well.
— Mine did, I know, — but still with heavier
      brains,
And wills more consciously responsible,
And not as wisely, since less foolishly;
So mothers have God's license to be missed.

Elizabeth Barrett Browning

168

CHILD AND MOTHER

O Mother-My-Love, if you'll give me your
  hand,
  And go where I ask you to wander,
I will lead you away to a beautiful land —
  The Dreamland that's waiting out yon-
    der.
We'll walk in a sweet-posie garden out there
  Where moonlight and starlight are stream-
    ing
And the flowers and birds are filling the
  air
  With fragrance and music of dreaming.

There'll be no little tired-out boy to undress,
  No questions or cares to perplex you;
There'll be no little bruises or bumps to
  caress,
  Nor patching of stockings to vex you.
For I'll rock you away on a silver-dew
  stream,
  And sing you asleep when you're weary,
And no one shall know of our beautiful
  dream
  But you and your own little dearie.

And when I am tired I'll nestle my head
  In the bosom that's soothed me so often,

And the wide-awake stars shall sing in my
stead
A song which our dreaming shall soften.
So Mother-my-Love, let me take your dear
hand,
And away through the starlight we 'll
wander —
Away through the mist to the beautiful
land —
The Dreamland that 's waiting out yon-
der!

Eugene Field

MY AIN WIFE

I WADNA gi'e my ain wife
For ony wife I see ;
I wadna gi'e my ain wife
For ony wife I see ;
A bonnier yet I 've never seen,
A better canna be —
I wadna gi'e my ain wife
For ony wife I see !

O couthie is my ingle-cheek,
An' cheerie is my Jean ;
I never see her angry look,
Nor hear her word on ane.
She 's gude wi' a' the neebours roun'
An' aye gude wi' me —

I wadna gi'e my ain wife
    For ony wife I see.

An' O her looks sae kindlie,
    They melt my heart outright,
When o'er the baby at her breast
    She hangs wi' fond delight;
She looks intill its bonnie face,
    An' syne looks to me —
I wadna gi'e my ain wife
    For ony wife I see.

Alexander Laing

SHE WAS A PHANTOM OF
DELIGHT

SHE was a phantom of delight
When first she gleamed upon my sight;
A lovely apparition, sent
To be a moment's ornament;
Her eyes as stars of twilight fair;
Like twilight's, too, her dusky hair;
But all things else about her drawn
From May-time and the cheerful dawn;
A dancing shape, an image gay,
To haunt, to startle, and waylay.

I saw her upon nearer view,
A spirit, yet a woman too!

To Mother

Her household motions light and free,
And steps of virgin liberty;
A countenance in which did meet
Sweet records, promises as sweet;
A creature not too bright or good
For human nature's daily food,
For transient sorrows, simple wiles,
Praise, blame, love, kisses, tears, and smiles.

And now I see with eye serene
The very pulse of the machine;
A being breathing thoughtful breath,
A traveler between life and death;
The reason firm, the temperate will,
Endurance, foresight, strength, and skill;
A perfect woman, nobly planned
To warn, to comfort, and command;
And yet a spirit still, and bright
With something of an angel light.

William Wordsworth

CLING TO THY MOTHER

CLING to thy mother; for she was the first
    To know thy being, and to feel thy life;
The hope of thee through many a pang she
        nurst;
    And when, midst anguish like the parting
        strife,

Her babe was in her arms, the agony
Was all forgot, for bliss of loving thee.

Be gentle to thy mother; long she bore
  Thine infant fretfulness and silly youth;
Nor rudely scorn the faithful voice that o'er
  Thy cradle pray'd, and taught thy lisp-
      ings truth.
Yes, she is old; yet on thine adult brow
She looks, and claims thee as her child e'en
    now.

Uphold thy mother; close to her warm heart
  She carried, fed thee, lull'd thee to thy
      rest;
Then taught thy tottering limbs their un-
    tried art,
  Exulting in the fledging from her nest;
And now her steps are feeble, by her stay,
Whose strength was thine in thy most feeble
    day.

Cherish thy mother; brief perchance the
    time
  May be that she will claim the care she
      gave;
Past are her hopes of youth, her harvest
    prime
  Of joy on earth; her friends are in the
      grave;

But for her children, she could lay her head
  Gladly to rest among her precious dead.

Be tender with thy mother; words unkind,
    Or light neglect from thee, will give a
        pang
To that fond bosom, where thou art en-
        shrined
    In love unutterable, more than fang
Of venom'd serpent. Wound not that strong
        trust
As thou wouldst hope for peace when she is
        dust.

O mother mine! God grant I ne'er forget,
    Whatever be my grief, or what my joy,
The unmeasured, inextinguishable debt
    I owe thy love; but make my sweet em-
        ploy
Ever through thy remaining days to be
To thee as faithful, as thou wert to me.
                              George Bethune

NOW I LAY ME DOWN TO SLEEP

" Now I lay me down to sleep:
  I pray the Lord my soul to keep,"
  Was my childhood's early prayer
  Taught by my mother's love and care.

Many years since then have fled ;
Mother slumbers with the dead ;
Yet methinks I see her now,
With love-lit eyes and holy brow,
As, kneeling by her side to pray,
She gently taught me how to say,
" Now I lay me down to sleep:
I pray the Lord my soul to keep."

Oh ! could the faith of childhood's days
Oh ! could its little hymns of praise,
Oh ! could its simple, joyous trust
Be recreated from the dust
That lies around a wasted life,
The fruit of many a bitter strife !
Oh ! then at night in prayer I 'd bend,
And call my God, my Father, Friend,
And pray with childlike faith once more
The prayer my mother taught of yore, —
" Now I lay me down to sleep:
I pray the Lord my soul to keep."

Eugene Henry Pullen

BIRTH

Just when each bud was big with bloom,
    And as prophetic of perfume,
When spring, with her bright horoscope,
    Was sweet as an unuttered hope ;

To Mother

Just when the last star flickered out,
  And twilight, like a soul in doubt,
Hovered between the dark and dawn,
  And day lay waiting to be born;

Just when the gray and dewy air
  Grew sacred as an unvoiced prayer,
And somewhere through the dusk she heard
  The stirring of a nested bird, —

Four angels glorified the place:
  Wan Pain unveiled her awful face;
Joy, soaring, sang; Love, brooding, smiled;
  Peace laid upon her breast a child.
      Annie R. Stillman ("Grace Raymond")

ONLY ONE

HUNDREDS of stars in the pretty sky;
  Hundreds of shells on the shore together;
Hundreds of birds that go singing by;
  Hundreds of bees in the sunny weather.

Hundreds of dewdrops to greet the dawn;
  Hundreds of lambs in the purple clover;
Hundreds of butterflies on the lawn;
  But only one mother the wide world over.
      George Cooper

"THE OLD FACE OF THE MOTHER OF MANY CHILDREN"

THE old face of the mother of many children,
Whist! I am fully content.

Lull'd and late is the smoke of the First-day
    morning,
It hangs low over the rows of trees by the
    fences,
It hangs thin by the sassafras and wild-
    cherry and cat-brier under them.

I saw the rich ladies in full dress at the
    soiree,
I heard what the singers were singing so
    long,
Heard who sprang in crimson youth from
    the white froth and the Water-blue.

Behold a woman!
She looks out from her Quaker cap, her face
    is clearer and more beautiful than the
    sky.

She sits in an armchair under the shaded
    porch of the farmhouse,
The sun just shines on her old white head.

To Mother

Her ample gown is of cream-hued linen,
Her grandsons raised the flax, and her grand-
    daughters spun it with the distaff and
    the wheel.

The melodious character of the earth,
The finish beyond which philosophy cannot
    go and does not wish to go,
The justified mother of men.

Walt Whitman

A MOTHER

AH! bless'd are they for whom, 'mid all
    their pains,
That faithful and unalter'd love remains;
Who, Life wreck'd round them — hunted
    from their rest —
And, by all else forsaken or distress'd —
Claim, in *one* heart, their sanctuary and
    shrine —
As I, my Mother, claim'd my place in
    thine !
Oft, since that hour, in sadness I retrace
My childhood's vision of thy calm sweet
    face ;
Oft see thy form, its mournful beauty
    shrouded
  In thy black weeds, and coif of widow's
    woe ;

Thy dark expressive eyes all dim and clouded
 By that deep wretchedness the lonely
  know:
Stifling thy grief, to hear some weary task,
 Conn'd by unwilling lips, with listless air;
Hoarding thy means, lest future need might
  ask
 More than the widow's pittance then could
  spare.
Hidden, forgotten by the great and gay,
 Enduring sorrow, not by fits and starts,
But the long self-denial, day by day,
 Alone amidst thy brood of careless hearts!
Striving to guide, to teach, or to restrain,
 The young rebellious spirits crowding
  round,
Who saw not, knew not, felt not for thy
  pain,
 And could not comfort — yet had power
  to wound!
Ah! how my selfish heart, which since hath
  grown
Familiar with deep trials of its own,
With riper judgment looking to the past,
Regrets the careless days that flew so fast,
Stamps with remorse each wasted hour of
  time,
And darkens every folly into crime!
Caroline E. S. Norton

TO MY MOTHER

I SEE your face as on that calmer day
When from my infant eyes it passed away
  Beyond these petty cares and questionings
  Beyond this sphere of sordid human
      things —
The trampled field of time's capricious play.

Bright with more mother-love than tongue
      can say,
Stern with the sense of foes in strong array,
  Yet hopeful, with no hopefulness earth
      brings —
    I see your face.

O gracious guarder from the primrose way,
O loving guide when wayward feet would
      stray,
  O inspiration sweet when the heart sings,
  O patient ministrant to sufferings,
Down the long road, *madonna mia*, may
    I see your face.

           Robert Haven Schauffler

MY MOTHER

SHE was as good as goodness is,
Her acts and all her words were kind,
And high above all memories
I hold the beauty of her mind.

           Frederic Hentz Adams

INDEX OF TITLES

Index of Titles

182

Index of Titles

Index of Titles

INDEX OF AUTHORS

Index of Authors

186